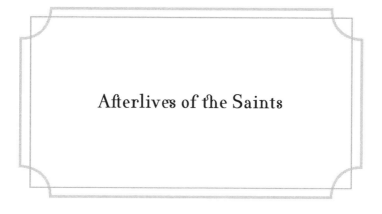

Afterlives of the Saints

Afterlives of the Saints

Stories from the Ends of Faith

COLIN DICKEY

UNBRIDLED BOOKS

Unbridled Books

Library of Congress Cataloging-in-Publication Data

Dickey, Colin.
Afterlives of the saints / Colin Dickey.
p. cm.
Summary: "Afterlives of the Saints is a woven gathering of groundbreaking essays
that move through Renaissance anatomy and the Sistine Chapel, Borges' "Library of
Babel," the history of spontaneous human combustion, the dangers of masturbation,
the pleasures of castration, "and so forth"—each essay focusing on the story of a
particular (and particularly strange) saint"—Provided by publisher.
ISBN 978-1-60953-072-3 (hardback)
1. Christian saints—Biography—Miscellanea. I. Title.
BR1710.D53 2012
270.092'2—dc23
[B]
2011046236

1 3 5 7 9 10 8 6 4 2

BOOK DESIGN BY SH * CV

First Printing

Contents

Part Thræ: An Indelicate Eros

Part Four: Demons of Belief

Part Five: The Uncanonized

List of Figures

For Nicole

As I continue to follow the march of history I recount
for you at one and the same time, and in the muddled
and confused order in which these events occurred,
the holy deeds of the Saints and the way in which
whole races of people were butchered.

—Gregory of Tours

Sainthood itself is not interesting, only the lives
of the saints.

—E. M. Cioran

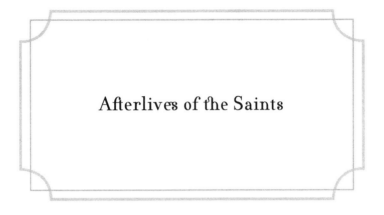

Afterlives of the Saints

Prologue:
The Earth's Rejects

On May 21, 2011, the entertainer Hezi Dean was hoisted to the top of a specially constructed ten-story pillar in the middle of Rabin Square in Tel Aviv. His goal was to stay there for the next thirty-five hours, in order to outlast the magician David Blaine, who had accomplished a similar feat in Central Park nine years earlier. Dean met his goal, beating Blaine's time and then jumping, as Blaine had done, onto a waiting pile of cardboard. Afterward, Dean told reporters, "It was very hard. I want to tell you only one important sentence: Nothing stands in front of the will."

Though Dean outlasted Blaine, he could hardly be said to be the record holder when it came to standing on tall pillars for long periods of time. That record, it turns out, has been unbroken for over a thousand years, and neither Blaine nor Dean came even close to touching it, for in the early fifth century, a saint named Simeon walked out into the Syrian desert, found an abandoned pillar, and climbed to the top of it. He stayed there not for thirty-five days but for thirty-seven years.

The first time I heard of Simeon, I was an undergraduate in a Western civilization class, and my professor made an offhand reference to strange Christian saints who would "go out in the desert and stand on poles and have people throw bread up to them." It was around this time that I first read the writings of Gregory of Tours, who ate the dust off the ground of Saint Martin's tomb. I first read of the horrific self-mutilations of Saint Radegund around then, too. And then I began collecting these stories—the bizarre miracles of Saint Foy, known as her "jokes"; the gallows humor of Lawrence, which earned him the title of patron saint of comedians; the torture of Bartholomew, flayed alive, which led to his becoming the patron of cheese-makers. Though I'd gone to a Catholic high school, these stories seemed very different, an alternative history of early religions and nations. It was through the saints, you could say, that I first began to understand that history is not a solid, purposeful arc from the darkness of the early ages to the enlightened modern era. It is, instead, full of strange detours, odd obsessions, embarrassments that were often meant to be forgotten.

Looking at the history of the saints is a bit like looking at a cliff's face: You can see an unbroken wall of rock, smooth and timeless, or you can read it as a geologist would, tracing the striations, the vestiges of geological epochs, an entire history of dynamic change that only slowly formed into the unmovable thing before you. So, too, with the saints; you can read them all as separate manifestations of the same unalterable divine moment, or you can read them as a long history of endlessly changing, constantly shifting expressions of faith. As I've collected stories of these strange saints over the years, what has repeatedly struck me is how far they seem to deviate from what most of us understand to be orthodoxy—these are saints who murder, saints who gouged out their own eyes and hold them out for inspection, saints who minister to the petty and the bizarre and the maligned. Put another way, the history of these saints helps enlarge our concept of faith. It was this realization that spurred the making of this book.

Saint Simeon never spread the gospel in a foreign, dangerous land, and he didn't spend his life devoted to charity and improving the life of his fellow humans. He was not martyred for his faith. He became a saint simply for standing on a pole in the desert for a really long time, which says as much about the time he lived in as about his current reputation. He was born in the Syrian town of Sis around 390 C.E. and joined a monastery when he was sixteen. He took to the monastic life and its deprivations immediately, but he didn't get along well with the other monks. Eager to prove his soul's purity and his scorn for his physical body, he took to waiting until the rest of the monks had gone to sleep and then hanging a heavy stone around his neck to stand vigil all night long. He sought a mastery of his own body, a denial of basic needs like sleep, as proof that his spiritual self was superior to his physical self. But it didn't always work; annoyed that his body, in its weakness, would occasionally fall asleep, Simeon started standing on a small wood log so that if he fell asleep he'd fall off and wake up. It was this behavior that finally alerted the other monks to what he was doing. Bothered by his excessive piety, which they thought bordered on hubris, they asked him to leave.

He ended up in Antioch and gradually became famous as a holy man. He attracted so much attention that, weary of the constant crowds, Simeon wandered out into the desert, where he found the column he first mounted. He eventually moved to increasingly higher posts and spent the last thirty years of his life on a pillar more than sixty feet high. Unlike Blaine or Dean, he did not have a catheter to handle bodily needs; one church historian described excrement running down the side of Simeon's pillar "like wax dripping down a candle." He stayed there until he died.

Simeon was not alone; there are records of at least ten other saints who were revered for standing on poles, including Alyspius, who had two smaller pillars constructed on each side of him for those seeking his counsel (one for monks and one for nuns), and may have even outlasted Simeon's record (contemporary sources claim he was up there for about fifty years). These ascetics were known as "stylites," from the Greek *stylos*, meaning pillar or column—the pole sitters. But even as more and more hermits climbed atop pillars to escape the world, Simeon, the first of them, remained the most well known, the originator of a strange craze that swept the desert in the fifth and sixth centuries.

Temperatures in the Syrian desert can get down into the 40s in the winter; there are stories of one stylite who was found covered in frost after three cold days—brought down from his pillar, he was found to still be very much alive. In February and March come the rains, followed by sandstorms. And then comes the summer, when the temperature ranges from a low of 104 to highs in excess of 113 degrees Fahrenheit.

At that temperature, the arteries begin to dilate in order to help dissipate the heat, which leads to a drop in blood pressure. The heart beats faster, trying to keep up, but as the body continues to lose water through dehydration, blood pressure drops further. Fainting, confusion, and hallucinations are common; in addition, the dilated blood vessels can allow for the accumulation of fluid just under the skin, a potentially dangerous condition once known as dropsy. Muscles contract unexpectedly and stay rigid; the body goes into shock.

But modern medical literature can only tell us so much about the stylites. Even having read the multiple stories—some firsthand—of these pole sitters, it seems simply inconceivable to me that a person, poorly hydrated and malnourished, could last even a few weeks exposed to such conditions, let alone several decades. Perhaps the stories are just fanciful exaggeration. Perhaps Simeon and the others survived due to some extremely rare and lucky constitutions or due to some fluke of physiology. Perhaps it was a miracle.

I don't know what really happened, and I've decided that it's not worth asking these questions. You can't treat a saint as you would an ordinary human. When I think of the saints, what comes to mind are the "replicants" in Ridley Scott's 1982 science fiction classic *Blade Runner*, androids of advanced strength and intelligence whom their creator describes as "more human than human."

This is the phrase that always comes to my mind when I think of the saints. Unlike the Christ, they are not divine, though divinity may pass through them. They may be miraculous, but even so they remain fully, stubbornly mortal. But while they participate in a common humanity, they lie at the very limit of that humanity— they have pushed what it means to be human to the breaking point, and then beyond. They have taken their own humanity and shattered it.

As with replicants, there's something dangerous about the saints. To see someone standing on a pole for thirty-five hours is to be impressed; to think of someone standing on a pole for thirty-seven years is to question all notions of will and self, devotion and sanity. Imagine for a moment what you've done in the past thirty-seven years—the cities, countries, continents you've visited; the jobs you've held; the accomplishments you could list; the lives of your children. Then imagine the gesture that renders all of that meaningless, that replaces it with a few motions: sitting, standing, eating, shitting. Praying. We know of repressive regimes that have forced such horrors on dissidents and other prisoners, but willfully to impose that obliteration on oneself for so long seems beyond comprehension.

In *Blade Runner*, the replicants are dangerous *because* they're perfect. They are a threat because they reveal our own limitations, our own obsolescence. It's why they have a four-year lifespan built in, why they're banned from Earth and hunted by crusaders like Harrison Ford's Lieutenant Deckard. Perfection is dangerous; it terrifies ordinary humans. What Deckard learns as he hunts down these replicants is that the line between human and more-than-human is elusive and that it's impossible to know for sure on which side each of us falls.

The renegade replicants in *Blade Runner* become violent because they are rapidly reaching the end of their four-year life spans, and they're desperate to extend their lives in any way possible. The saints, however, desire the opposite. They don't want more life; they want more death. In a 2005 interview, the novelist Mary Gordon described her memories of the path to sainthood in the 1950s:

I remember, before we were being prepared for our first communion, we would be six or seven, we were told that we should pray for a martyr's death. So you would have these seven year olds saying, "Oh my God I better pray that . . . a Communist will say, 'Either say there is no God or we'll shoot you.'" . . . [So] when I was about nine or ten, I would put thorns in my shoes, to try to walk around, to experience the preliminaries of martyrdom, so I'd be toughened up for the real thing.

In a religion centered around a God who willingly allowed Himself to be crucified, the idea of a martyr's death has always been important. The chance to die, to be rid of one's body, all the while affirming one's faith, was nothing short of a gift. Christianity isn't unique in this, of course; Gordon's childhood memories echo those of the Japanese writer Kenzaburo Oē, who was born in the years before World War II and underwent similar indoctrination. Called to the front of the classroom, like all Japanese schoolchildren, Oē was asked, "What would you do if the emperor commanded you to die?" The young boy replied, knees shaking, "I would die, sir; I would cut open my belly and die."

Neither Gordon nor Oē, both just children, really wanted to die. Gordon recalled how, even with thorns in her shoes, "I didn't want my feet to hurt, so I would put the thorns in my shoes, then I'd try not to step on them. So it was a sort of equivocal appetite for martyrdom, and nonetheless always feeling that I wasn't quite up to scratch, because I wanted to live, I didn't want to die." But that is what it means to love a divinity: to crave death, to want to die daily, to reject this world in favor of the promise of another. It's why most of us aren't cut out to be saints, why many of us find something fairly unhealthy about the very idea. To be a saint is to see one's body as nothing more than a chance to demonstrate that love of death.

After the Roman emperor Constantine legalized Christianity in 313, there was no longer an easy and straight path to martyrdom. Without persecution, torture, and execution, many saints turned to self-inflicted punishment: self-flagellation, deprivation, asceticism. "I have no greater enemy than my body," Francis of Assisi wrote. "We should feel hatred for our body, for its vices and sinning." But few still consider this mode of worship through extreme physical self-torment holy, and this kind of extreme vocation represented by the saints is hardly to be celebrated. Even while Pope John Paul II was (according to some sources) privately whipping himself, he publicly preached the sacredness of the human body and the need to respect it.

The saint's hatred of the mortal body, after all, entails a recklessness bordering on the suicidal. One of Italy's patron saints, the fourteenth-century Catherine of Siena, regularly shoved branches down her throat to make herself vomit the meager food she ate (a process she called "retribution") and was ultimately killed by this holy anorexia, dying of malnutrition and thirst at the age of thirty-three.

The saints, one realizes, are to be revered but not imitated. They're there to show us how to be human by being what we could never be.

Simeon the Stylite chose his own mode of self-punishment in part because of its symbolic value: Standing on a column, he was elevated, above the world literally and figuratively, yearning for heaven and for God. It was because of this that other hermits followed his example, and why living atop a pole became a particularly popular form of asceticism for hundreds of years. It was a very visible metaphor, clearly announcing one's devotion to heaven.

At the same time, Simeon's gesture announced his rejection of the ground below, and for this reason many commentators since have been particularly derisive toward the stylites. In *The History of the Decline and Fall of the Roman Empire*, the nineteenth-century British historian Edward Gibbon had nothing but scorn for Simeon and his asceticism: "This voluntary martyr-dom must have gradually destroyed the sensibility both of the mind and the body," he noted, going on to claim, "nor can it be presumed that the fanatics who torment themselves are susceptible of any lively affection for the rest of mankind." For Gibbon, the crime of an ascetic like Simeon is the implied narcissism in such a renunciation of the world, an internal struggle at the expense of a life of charity.

Gibbon had a strong contempt for Christianity, blaming its

spread for the decline of the empire that had once tried to eradicate it, so his distaste for Simeon is not surprising—but beyond his personal aversion to the desert saint, his comments came at a time when attitudes toward ascetics were turning from awe to contempt and pity. It was Gibbon's account of Simeon, along with that in William Hone's *Every-Day Book*, that inspired Alfred, Lord Tennyson, to write a long, dramatic monologue from the saint's perspective in 1833. "The watcher on the column till the end," Simeon calls himself in Tennyson's poem, one "unfit for earth, unfit for heaven." The saints belong to both worlds, but in occupying that strange halfway position, they paradoxically belong to neither. Unlike angels, their home is not in heaven; unlike Jesus, they are not on loan. They are Earth's rejects; they have no real place here and so spend their time with their eyes watching God.

As he surveys his final hours, Tennyson's Simeon is plagued with doubt. Rather than speaking as a figure of certainty and piety, he's unsure whether he's earned sainthood, or even if anyone has witnessed his devotion.

O Jesus, if thou wilt not save my soul,
Who may be saved? who is it may be saved?
Who may be made a saint, if I fail here?
Show me the man hath suffer'd more than I.
For did not all thy martyrs die one death?
For either they were stoned, or crucified,

Or burn'd in fire, or boil'd in oil, or sawn
In twain beneath the ribs; but I die here
To-day, and whole years long, a life of death.

Simeon became a saint not because of his good works or his martyrdom but because he outmartyred the martyrs. He didn't die; he turned his life into death. "A life of death": This is the true vocation of the saint—the walking dead, zombies in their faith.

O ver a hundred years after Tennyson's poem, the Spanish director Luis Buñuel revisited the saint's legend with his film *Simon of the Desert*, in which a similarly named stylite and his trials embody all the failings Buñuel perceived in the Catholic Church. Buñuel's steadfast Simon is beset by peasants who plead for relief and offer no gratitude, or even surprise, in the face of Simon's miracles; he is surrounded by bickering monks whose banal concerns create an endless babble of noise beneath his pillar; and he is tormented by a low-rent Satan (played by Silvia Pinal), who seems to tempt Simon mostly out of boredom. Simon, the straight man to this absurdity, remains pious, if sometimes exasperated— yet it's clear that his refusal to engage with the world has itself become part of the problem.

For Buñuel, as for Tennyson, the saints are not just more than human; they are also less than human: cast off and exiled, marginal figures on the border of ridicule for their absurd failures to live among us. But even so, the hermit himself is not Buñuel's target. As the film critic Michael Wood notes, "what's worse than ridiculous, in Buñuel's view, is the religion that has taken this man's life away from him, the service of that God who never dies. Simon is neither the first nor the last to abandon the intricate human world for the sake of an extreme idea; and his crazy, admirable virtue is part of the problem because it is admirable as well as crazy."

Buñuel fought a lifelong struggle against the Catholic Church and what he perceived as its backward thinking and hypocrisy, but, as Wood notes, "God can't ultimately condemn serious atheists. They pay far more attention to him than halfhearted believers do, and they help to keep him in business." Buñuel is closer to Milton than he is to the average churchgoer because, despite his derision, he remains deadly serious. He knows the stakes, and he takes his adversary seriously. In films like *Belle du Jour* and *Viridiana*, Buñuel takes aim at those who are repressed by decorum and religion, unable to free their desires. He despises the saint's piety but not his excesses. Indeed, Buñuel's cynicism hides a desire for that excess, for a life lived at the margins.

Like Buñuel, I am less interested in the piety of the saints than in their excesses, their madness, their inability to live normal lives. I want to open up the meaning of the saint. I want to see what moves at the margins; I want to push at the boundaries of the human until something gives way.

W̶e now live in a world far less tolerant of such extremes, which is why, perhaps, it has become so compelling to revisit the saints in a contemporary context. Buñuel's film ends in the city, as the fifth-century saint is miraculously transported via a jetliner to an unnamed metropolis and deposited in a nightclub, where young kids are dancing something called "Radioactive Flesh." It's the "final dance," Silvia Pinal's Satan tells Simon: "You'll have to stick it out. You'll have to stick it out until the end."

Gustave Flaubert, too, who spent his life trying to write a book based on the life of Saint Anthony, ended one draft in a city where Anthony walks through an urbanscape where "smoke escapes from the houses, tongues of fire twist upwards in the dense air. Iron bridges span rivers of filth; carriages, sealed as tightly as coffins, encumber the long, straight streets." The temptation to strand the saint in the modern city comes perhaps from the fact that saints no longer belong there. Though there are modern saints, the idea of a saint is *always* anachronistic—an occupation from another time that has no real corollary in contemporary life.

"At the base of a stylite's pillar," the English writer William Dalrymple notes, "one is confronted with the awkward truth that what has moved past generations can today sometimes be only tentatively glimpsed with the eye of faith, while remaining quite inexplicable and absurd when seen under the harsh distorting microscope of sceptical Western rationality." A modern ascetic risks being labeled with all manner of clinical diagnoses: Masochism, anorexia, schizophrenia—those former paths to sainthood nowadays run straight through the DSM IV and psychopharmacology. In short, those old obsessions are incompatible with modern life, which sees them as pathologies that interrupt a productive life. The saints have become, in Buñuel's words, "singular individuals who are placed at the margin of history, of daily life, and all because of a fixed idea."

Perhaps these fixed obsessions are why I find the writings of the saints so fascinating. There's a simplicity in their writing that reduces the entire world, all of lived experience, to a single idea, a locus from which everything else must be seen. Whether it's Gregory of Tours narrating the history of time and space or Teresa of Avila narrating her ecstatic visions, the writings of the saints all revolve around a singular, divine moment.

If we can no longer experience the world through an extreme lens, as did the saints who once walked among us, with their bodies pushed to the limits, then the best we can hope for is a parallel experience in art. Tennyson and Buñuel were not alone in turning to this subject matter; many artists and writers have found their muses in the saints, from atheists like Buñuel and Flaubert to more reverential artists like Caravaggio or Georges de La Tour. The saints have become a creative engine by which artists can tap into bloody excess, a kind of superhuman insanity. If I follow in their footsteps, it is not as a theologian but as one more writer trying to learn something about my own time by retelling these stories once more.

Hagiography—the writing of the lives of the saints—is a curious genre, now mostly forgotten. Take, for example, the life of the Belgian saint Vincent Madelgarus, who died in 677. When an unknown priest set out to write his story, he began by copying the prologue from the life of Saint Erminus, followed by a second prologue stolen word for word from Gregory of Tours's life of Saint Patroclus. The story of Vincent's marriage is also stolen, this time from Gregory's life of Saint Leobard, as is a divine vision Vincent experiences and the description of his son, Landric. His decision to embrace the ascetic life is borrowed, exactly, from the life of Saint Bavon, and his death is also a reworking of the death of another, Saint Ursmar.

In this hagiography, Saint Vincent Madelgarus is nothing more than a collage of plagiarized sources, a seventh-century version of sampling. And this is by no means the only case of such plagiarism; the hagiographies of Saint Lambert and Saint Remaclus are identical, and there's so much overlap between the lives of Hubert and Arnold of Metz that modern historians are at a loss as to which event happened to whom.

Plagiarism was common among early writers of hagiography, who would not have understood the term *plagiarism* anyway. If Eddius's *Life of Saint Wilfred* steals from Evagrius's *Life of Saint*

Anthony, which in turn took material from Sulpicus's *Life of Saint Martin*, the point was the grand scheme of perfection that lay behind all these lives and all these stories. Hagiographers prized not the individual details of one's life but the universals, the commonalities. The abbot Bede, who had known Saint Cuthbert personally, wrote an eighty-five page narrative of his life but went out of his way to eliminate any factual detail, any specific point of reference, any historical location or date. Anything that would ground Cuthbert as a real person who lived in a real time and place was excised.

It's not that a writer like Bede was lazy or didn't have his facts straight. Rather, as a hagiographer, he had a specific goal. He and other writers *wanted* to make the saints look the same. In hagiography, the story is written to tell us not the facts about that person's life but rather how that person's life exemplifies the glory of God. The true protagonist of the hagiography is never the saint; the true protagonist is always just offstage, in His heaven.

As I began writing the stories that became this book, I wanted to avoid precisely this approach to these lives. I wanted to find their individuality and the unique legacies that they left to the world they sought to change.

There are thousands of saints, and no book could hope to treat them all. I haven't tried: The saints in these pages are only a tiny fragment of the many to be written about. But they are the ones who have spoken most to me over the years, either because of what they wrote (Part One), because of the art and literature they inspired (Parts Two and Three), or because of the wide range of beliefs they encompassed (Part Four). Finally there are those who were never formally recognized as saints but whose lives and actions speak to the divine in all of us.

"Sainthood itself is not interesting, only the lives of the saints," the philosopher E. M. Cioran once wrote. I, too, am uninterested in writing that downplays the humanity of the saint in favor of God's divinity. For me, saints exist not as a medium for God but as a lens for humanity.

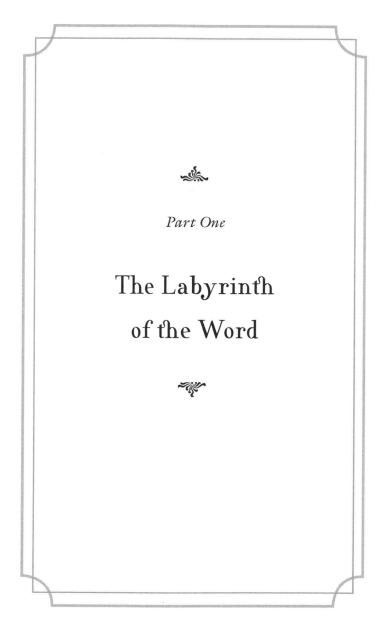

Part One

The Labyrinth
of the Word

FIGURE 1: *Scene from the Apocalypse, the Opening of the Fifth and Sixth Seals* (1511), Albrecht Dürer. BIBLIOTHEQUE NATIONALE, PARIS, FRANCE/GIRAUDON/THE BRIDGEMAN ART LIBRARY

ONE

The Singer at the
End of the World:
Gregory of Tours

This is how the end of the world looked in the sixth century: In Gaul, above the River Rhône, a "curious bellowing sound" was heard for sixty days before a hillside collapsed. In Auvergne in 571, a plague that decimated the population was preceded by "three or four great shining lights" that hovered around the sun. There were eclipses and comets and birds that flew into churches, miraculously extinguishing every candle "so quickly that you would have thought that someone had seized hold of them all at once and dropped them into a pool of water." On November 11, 578, during a celebration of mass in Tours, "a bright star shining in the very center of the moon" appeared. In 580, floods devastated the region, and a sound "as of trees crashing to the ground" was heard for fifty miles in every direction.

The signs were everywhere. A fire in Paris in 585 burned everything but the churches of Saint Martin and Saint Germanus. In the ruins, a mysterious bronze statue of a snake and a rat was found; when it was removed, the city became infested with snakes and rats for the first time. In April 586, an epidemic decimated Tours and Nantes, death proceeding rapidly from a slight headache. In the town of Limoges, those conducting business on the Sabbath were consumed by fire, while elsewhere in France a drought destroyed acres of farmland. Men sold themselves into slavery to get something to eat. In Chartres, people discovered their jars inscribed with characters they could neither remove nor read. Shortly thereafter, new grapevine shoots appeared mysteriously in October, along with deformed grapes. Flashes of light shot out from blood-red clouds; snakes dropped from the sky; entire villages disappeared.

The Messiah appeared and reappeared, and reappeared. A man named Desiderus emerged in Tours in 587, calling himself the Savior and offering to cure the paralyzed and the crippled, forcibly stretching out their bodies as he called on his divine power; those he did not cure were sent away, half dead and broken. In Gaul, plague broke out, and during the epidemic a woodcutter was attacked by a swarm of flies, went insane, and proclaimed himself Christ. He attracted some three thousand followers and began his own plague of banditry: He and his followers robbed everyone who passed on the road and gave what they took to the poor. After a few months, he took his army to lay siege to the cathedral; once he was there, the bishop sent out emissaries claiming to be peace envoys—when they reached this Christ, they summarily executed him and dispersed his followers, torturing any who remained.

Another man claiming to be Christ was arrested and jailed without protest. Shortly thereafter he broke out and escaped to the local monastery, whereupon he promptly passed out, dead drunk. When the bishop of Tours found him the next morning, he smelled so bad the bishop could not stand to go near him. Unable to get his attention, he tried to wake this Messiah by singing as loudly as he could.

Let your first image of Gregory be this: singing hymns one morning in 580 to a passed-out Christ. Imagine him the singer, singing the end of the world.

Gregory was a diminutive man, short enough to have been mocked for it by the pope. Beyond that, though, is a humility that comes across in his writing and that makes his books a pleasure to read. He was the descendent of bishops, popes, and senators, and in 573 he found himself in charge of the important bishopric of Tours, where Saint Martin's tomb was located.

Important tombs were not only pilgrimage sites, they were also a major source of revenue as well as a source of miracles. Not just the relics but everything about the tomb of Saint Martin radiated magic. When Saint Aredius visited Martin's tomb, he gathered some dust in a box, which he took back to his monastery, but miraculously the dust "increased in quantity until it not only filled the box but forced its way through the joints wherever it could find an opening."

Gregory understood the power of such dust. In an age when disease rampaged unchecked and medicine was poorly understood, Gregory inoculated himself against everything from a cold to the plague by mixing the dust from Martin's tomb (along with a few other ground-up relics) into various elixirs and tonics. On more than one occasion, he reported, the miraculous dust saved his life, including the night before his ordination as bishop of Tours, when he said Martin's remains saved him from dysentery.

This is the second great image of Gregory: the dust eater.

G regory's masterpiece, *A History of the Franks*, has long struck me as analogous to epic modern novels, in particular Joyce's *Ulysses* and Proust's *In Search of Lost Time*. For Joyce and Proust, the goal was to take a single moment—a walk through Dublin, the taste of a madeleine—and explode it into a thousand pages, to take the nearly infinite layers of experience and lay them all out on the page.

Gregory similarly wanted to write the whole of human experience, but his method differs—rather than single out that one moment that could act as a microcosm, he set out to narrate the history of human experience from its dawn to its end. Gregory begins not with the origin of the Franks or his own life but with the beginning of the world; his book's original title was simply *Decem Libri Historiarum* (The ten books of history). Book I contains the Bible in paraphrase, and the line of history moves unbroken into Gregory's own time (starting in Book IV), the entire work offering a seamless progression of history from Adam and Eve to his own time.

He writes of the end of dynasties with remarkable lack of pity, as in his cool and objective account of King Lothar's ordering that his son Chramm along with Chramm's wife and daughters be burned alive. Just as easily he tells of close human dramas and the pain of learning of his own brother's murder. Gregory was close enough to the political intrigues of his time to see how behind-the-scenes machinations were set in motion, and he recorded the passing of the seasons with the detail of an almanac.

Numerical tallies end each of the ten books of his opus so that one can trace the exact record of days since Eden. "For the sake of those who are losing hope as they see the end of the world coming nearer and nearer," he writes, "I also think it desirable that, from material assembled from the chronicles and histories of earlier writers, I should explain clearly how many years have passed since the world began." One must start from the beginning, above all, because the end is imminent.

And with signs all around him, Gregory no doubt imagined his book was chronicling the end of days, just as he had narrated their beginning. Gregory's book is not cut from the cloth of time; it is the cloth entire.

But the odd thing about Gregory's book of history is that

the end never comes. Despite an exhaustive catalog of portents, omens, and unexplained signs, Gregory's world consistently fails to come to its conclusion. After seven hundred pages, his masterpiece ends on a curiously ambiguous, if not deflated, note: "Acorns grew," he tells us, "but they never ripened."

Even worse than T. S. Eliot's claim that the world ends with a whimper and not a bang is the truth that it doesn't end at all. No bang. No whimper. Only unripe acorns and the next day and the next.

Gregory's surprise that the world didn't end on his watch is a feeling too many of us share. We have a hard time believing the world will survive us. We have a hard time accepting that we are living in the middle of history. As Frank Kermode points out, humans are born in medias res, and we die before the final curtain. So we make "fictive concords with origins and ends" to give meaning to our lives. It is our tendency to take the unbroken span of time and organize it around the importance of our own moment: "We thrive on epochs," in Kermode's words. But these epochs, however elaborately defined, exist only as a psychological defense against the unavoidable fact that the world does not end with our own death—a reality as offensive as it is terrifying. "We are the middle children of history," says Tyler Durden in Chuck Palahniuk's *Fight Club*, and it is the very rage over this fact that drives the men in that novel first to self-targeted brutality and then to terrorism. We crave the apocalypse because the alternative seems worse.

The Labyrinth of the Word

It is out of a need to make epochs, to create fictive concords with origins and ends, that we write history. Writing history begins by cutting into the whole cloth that is time, choosing a beginning, narrating an arc. It's about finding a pattern, taking the raw facts of existence and making an argument from them. In history, Hayden White tells us, "reality wears the mask of a meaning, the completeness and fullness of which we can only *imagine*, never experience." Faced with the realization that history is unending, that it exists before us and continues after us, the historian can select only a sliver of time, designate a beginning and an end where none truly exists.

Gregory didn't have this problem—he lived when one could still conceive of all of history at once. Perhaps his was the last generation to be able to do so, to conceive of a book that contains both the alpha and the omega. Nowadays, to believe that the end is imminent requires both self-importance and ignorance; Gregory had neither. To him, it seemed, was entrusted the entire span of history. Even though we've outlived him, his book is like nothing else, the perfect and complete record of the mortal world.

But you and I live on the other side of this great divide, in a time now fragmented, unredeemed. When we look at the trajectory of human history, we see mostly the promises of apocalypses that never happened. Faced with all the calculations and predictions of the end in our time, perhaps it's best to remember Gregory's acorns that grew but never ripened.

⚛

There's a short Kafka fable, barely two pages long, about a strange creature who lives in an apartment hallway:

> At first glance it looks like a flat star-shaped spool for thread, and indeed it does seem to have thread wound upon it; to be sure, they are only old, broken-off bits of thread, knotted and tangled together, of the most varied sorts and colors. But it is not only a spool, for a small wooden crossbar sticks out of the middle of the star, and another small rod is joined to that at a right angle.

You might think this a description of a pile of trash, but no, it's a creature; it's alive; it's called Odradek: "By means of this latter rod on one side and one of the points of the star on the other, the whole thing can stand upright as if on two legs."

Odradek is harmless, devoid of malice, yet the title of Kafka's story, "Cares of a Family Man," suggests that Odradek's mere presence is somehow troubling. The family man of the story's title confesses that he is disturbed by Odradek, in part because he appears incomplete but is not:

> One is tempted to believe that the creature once had some sort of intelligible shape and is now only a broken-down remnant. Yet this does not seem to be the case; at least there is no sign of it; nowhere is there an unfinished

or unbroken surface to suggest anything of the kind; the whole thing looks senseless enough, but in its own way perfectly finished.

The real problem with Odradek is that he is useless, and because he is useless, he is also immortal:

> I ask myself, to no purpose, what is likely to happen to him? Can he possibly die? Anything that dies has had some kind of aim in life, some kind of activity, which has worn out; but that does not apply to Odradek. Am I to suppose, then, that he will always be rolling down the stairs, with ends of thread trailing after him, right before the feet of my children, and my children's children? He does no harm to anyone that one can see; but the idea that he is likely to survive me I find almost painful.

Sixty-seven years after Kafka's death, the artist Jeff Wall staged a photograph of a young girl descending a staircase in a run-down apartment building in Prague. Wearing a gaudy jacket of hot pink and bright yellow, she belongs firmly in the early 1990s, but huddled in the shadows of the stairs is an odd construction of wire, wood, and yarn. Titled *Odradek, Tàboritskà 8, Prague, 18 July 1994*, Wall's photograph shows what's lurking in the shadows of every apocalypse—the aimless, immortal Odradek. He is always with us, and that's what's so disturbing.

We want to believe that we can understand history as Gregory understood it—perfect, unbroken, guided by purpose. But a nagging fear too often creeps in—it is the purposeless and useless trash like Odradek that will inherit the earth. The cares of the family man are also our own.

If Gregory could believe that dust was holy enough to stave off death, then perhaps we, too, can learn to see magic in some cast-off thread and wood and metal, which seems a ruin of some great catastrophe but may in fact have its own beauty, complete in itself.

TWO

The Librarian's Dream: Jerome

G regory of Tours may be one of the greatest writers of the saints, but he is not the one most commonly associated with the Word itself. That honor goes to the saint of editing and collecting, of libraries, of bibliographies and *biblios*—Hieronymous, known commonly as Jerome.

If Gregory is God's perfect historian, Jerome is God's perfect librarian. Jerome became the patron saint of libraries and librarians because of the one task he is most known for: the translation, editing, and assemblage of what became the standard edition of the Bible for more than the first millennium—the Vulgate. Various canonical lists of the Bible had been circulating as early as the mid–third century, but only with the Council of Rome in 382 did an official council of bishops agree on the list of books to be included. Known as the Damasine List, it was named for Pope Damasus I, who headed the council and had hired Jerome as his personal secretary. And so it fell to Jerome, also present at the council, to assemble a fresh translation of this newly ratified library—known first as the *versio vulgata*, or commonly used translation, and later simply as the Vulgate.

For all the controversy surrounding the Bible, its apocrypha and conflicting versions, Jerome's accomplishment was seen in terms of divine intervention—as the Council of Rome had been guided by the hand of God, so Jerome must have been. Seen in this light, the Bible is perfect: There are no books missing, no books extraneous. It is a perfect library, a collection of exactly the books that God intended for humankind.

Every librarian since, one way or another, has been forced to measure her- or himself against this librarian saint. Anyone seeking to build the perfect collection must reckon at some point with the divine certainty of Jerome. And if you cannot be sure, as Jerome was, exactly what belongs in your library, then the only alternative is to include it all, leave nothing out. It was this caution that motivated Ptolemy I to build the Library of Alexandria at the end of the third century B.C.E., in which he hoped to assemble "all the books of all the people of the world." Ptolemy calculated all the books in the world to be roughly five hundred thousand volumes; this seemingly large number would now represent just a fraction of the total books in existence. Long ago, our capacity for books overtook any sane number: The complete library is now, quite simply, infinite. If you do not have the divine grace of Jerome to tell you which books to keep and which to exclude, you are obligated to take in everything, and you are condemned to a library without end.

This is the library imagined by Jorge Luis Borges in his short story "The Library of Babel." He describes the library as an "indefinite, perhaps infinite number of hexagonal galleries."

In the center of each gallery is a ventilation shaft, bounded by a low railing. From any hexagon one can see the floors above and below—one after another, endlessly. The arrangement of the galleries is always the same: Twenty bookshelves, five to each side, line four of the hexagon's six sides; the height of the bookshelves, floor to ceiling, is hardly greater than the height of a normal librarian. One of the hexagon's free sides opens onto a narrow sort of vestibule, which in turn opens onto another gallery, identical to the first—identical, in fact, to all. To the left and right of the vestibule are two tiny compartments. One is for sleeping, upright; the other, for satisfying one's physical necessities. Through this space, too, there passes a spiral staircase, which winds upward and downward into the remotest distance.

Every librarian, every book collector, finds him- or herself between these two mythical places—the Perfect Finite Library of

God and the Infinite Library of Babel, the one transcribed by Jerome, the other by Borges.

But in some ways, they are closer to one another than they first appear. Borges's description of the infinite library as a series of hexagonal cells that disappear into the distance echoes (perhaps coincidentally) the Roman catacombs that Jerome would visit while he was a young scholar, with bodies instead of books. "Often," he writes, "I would find myself entering those crypts, deep dug in the earth, with their walls on either side lined with the bodies of the dead. . . . Here and there," he continues, "the light, not entering in through windows, but filtering down from above through shafts, relieved the horror of the darkness. But again, as soon as you found yourself cautiously moving forward, the black night closed around and there came to my mind the line of Virgil, 'the horror and the silences terrified their souls.' "

It was to mortify his own soul that Jerome came down to those catacombs so that he could remind himself of his own mortality. This reminder of death—in Latin *memento mori*, "remember that you will die"—is represented in art by a human skull, the grinning death's head we all will leave behind. This skull is a common image in representations of Jerome, the saint who transcribes the immortal Word even as his mortal body fails him.

The most compelling of these images of Jerome are those by the Italian Renaissance painter Caravaggio. In one painting, he depicts the librarian's long, thin arm stretched out over a great folio, and on that folio—as a compositional counterpoint to Je-

rome's haloed head—rests a human skull, reminding him of what
awaits, exhorting him to prepare for the next life.

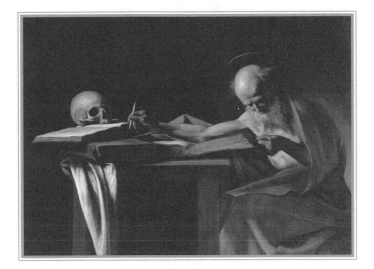

FIGURE 2: *Saint Jerome Writing* (c. 1604), Michelangelo
Merisi da Caravaggio GALLERIA BORGHESE, ROME, ITALY/
THE BRIDGEMAN ART LIBRARY

In Jerome's time, this preparation took the form of asceticism, a word deriving from the Greek *askesis,* which means "exer-
cise" or "athletic training." In practice, asceticism was abstinence
from worldly pleasures and all but the most basic needs—the deprivation of one's physical needs seen as crucial preparation for the
time when one was without body, when one was pure spirit. Caravaggio's painting of Jerome is striking because he so forcefully

emphasizes the decrepit, ailing body of the great librarian. Jerome is more skeletal than flesh, his arm stretched across the folio like a body pulled across the rack, as though the immortal Word were itself some kind of torture device.

Caravaggio reminds us that Jerome was not only a librarian; he was also flesh, mortal. There's a subversive element to Caravaggio's painting, precisely because what's most engaging about the work is Jerome's hated mortal coil, that which he cannot escape. Jerome began devoting himself to asceticism when he was about thirty years old, having left Rome for Antioch after a serious illness led him to abandon his remaining secular studies. He ventured into the deserts of Syria, where a converted Jew taught him Hebrew and he began translations of the Hebrew Scriptures. Eventually he returned to civilization and allowed himself to be ordained as a bishop, but only under the condition that he be allowed to maintain his ascetic life. Immersed in his books and his translations, Jerome prepared his body for death and prepared his mind for a life without his corruptible body.

Returning to Rome, Jerome was distinctly out of place—a desert hermit amid a bustling metropolis. He harangued the city's clergymen for their posh lifestyle, making himself more than a few enemies. But eventually a circle of wealthy women, including the widow Paula and her daughter Blaesilla, gravitated to him, following his example and adopting an ascetic lifestyle.

Here in Rome, under the direction of Damasus, the master librarian continued work on his perfect library, where his reading itself was a sort of asceticism. As Michel de Montaigne noted 1,400 years later, reading "is not a plain and pure pleasure . . . it has its disagreements, and they are onerous; the soul disports itself, but the body, whose care I have not forgotten, remains inactive, it grows weary and sad." In the very act of reading and study, Jerome could be said to be forever mortifying his body.

As I read my way through these accounts of his life, I found myself wondering if the very act of reading, or at least book collecting, was itself a kind of memento mori, and whether this is the reason so many scholars over the centuries have included human skulls in their libraries, perched amid their books on endless shelves. Like Jerome, Borges's unnamed librarian remains fixated on his own death. "I am preparing to die, a few leagues from the hexagon where I was born," he tells us early on. "When I am dead, compassionate hands will throw me over the railing; my tomb will be the unfathomable air, my body will sink for ages, and will decay and dissolve in the wind engendered by my fall, which shall be infinite."

That image is both beautiful and haunting, but I wonder: In the Library of Babel, do bones, too, decay? Borges's description suggests that they do, that at some point during the infinite fall even the librarian's bones disintegrate. But for a fall to be infinite, there must be something that is always falling, and I prefer to think that the bones remain, and that they fall infinitely, endlessly, through the hexagonal galleries, so that as the librarians go about their business in the Library of Babel, every so often comes the sound of bones from some librarian who died many, many floors up. The shafts of this great library filled with the sporadic clattering of bones, a memento mori falling at terminal velocity.

The stubborn reality of the body over the immortal Word was a truth that the widow Paula and her daughter Blaesilla were to learn all too well. After a few months following Jerome's ascetic lifestyle, Blaesilla, who had recently recovered from a serious illness, collapsed from exhaustion and malnutrition and died shortly thereafter. Paula was grief-stricken, but Jerome found her display of earthly emotion both unbecoming and unchristian. The master librarian chastised Paula for her grief at the loss of her daughter's earthly body: "I pardon you the tears of a mother, but I ask you to restrain your grief," he wrote to her. "When I think of the parent I cannot blame you for weeping: but when I think of the Christian and the recluse, the mother disappears from my view." Ultimately Jerome was forced out of Rome, in part because his protector, Damasus, died but also because of his indirect role in the death of Blaesilla and his cold indifference to her fate.

Before I read this story, I had always assumed, or wanted to believe, that the narrator in Borges's fable was a version of Jerome and that we were listening to the voice of the great librarian himself. But I'm less sure now. Late in the story, the narrator describes a librarian greater than himself whom he calls the Book-Man, the librarian who understands the entirety of the Library of Babel, the sole librarian who has read the ultimate book. "On some shelf in some hexagon," he says, "there must exist a book that is the cipher and perfect compendium *of all other books,* and some librarian must have examined that book." The Book-Man is thus clearly analogous to a god, but I would argue that Jerome is a better fit—after all, it is not God whom librarians dream of but Jerome. And if this longing for the perfect library sometimes takes the form of idolatry, so be it. Borges's narrator tells us that "there are still vestiges of the sect that worshipped that distant librarian. Many have gone in search of Him. For a hundred years, men beat every possible path—and every path in vain." And finally, Borges's narrator confesses that he, too, has long searched for the Book-Man:

> It is in ventures such as these that I have squandered and spent my years. I cannot think it unlikely that there is such a total book on some shelf in the universe. I pray to the unknown gods that some man—even a single man, tens of centuries ago—has perused and read that book. If the honor and wisdom and joy of such a reading are not to be my own, then let them be for others. Let heaven exist, though my own place be in hell. Let me be tortured and battered and annihilated, but let there be one instant, one creature, wherein thy enormous Library may find its justification.

Searching himself for the Book-Man, he is not Jerome, sure in the perfection of his work and in the smug knowledge of a library that is so perfect it needs neither our bodies nor our bones. He is instead Blaesilla, willing to pledge himself on faith and willing to annihilate himself in subservience to the secrets that the perfect librarian may hold.

THREE

Silencing the
Books: Paula

The seventeenth-century Christian philosopher Gottfried Leibniz saw the library as something like an analogy for the universe, which he used to explain the presence of evil in the world. Suppose there are two libraries, he tells us. One library consists of a thousand copies of the most perfect book, which for Leibniz was Virgil's *Aeneid*. The other library consists of a thousand different books—some are great; some are terrible. One of them is the *Aeneid*, but the other 999 books fail to reach its level of perfection.

Which of the two libraries is better? Of course, Leibniz knows it's the one with different books, even if not all of them are as great as Virgil's epic. In this way, he argues, we can understand

God's plan and the existence of pain and evil. We are all part of an endlessly diverse library of God, and we all participate in the glory of that diversity.

I first read this analogy in one of Borges's essays, where he calls it "elegant but false." Leibniz, Borges tells us, "seems to forget that it is one thing that *there are* bad books in the library, and another thing *to be* those books." And, he concludes, "if we are those books, we are condemned to hell." Borges reminds us that one cannot confuse books with people. This was the difficulty facing Saint Paula, mother of the dead Blaesilla and a constant companion to Jerome—the severe librarian who saw in her the perfect text, who made a book of her.

For the most part, Jerome thought the only good woman was a virgin. He understood women as belonging to three categories, and he ranked them accordingly: Virgins are "first-fruits," followed by widows and, finally, married women. For Jerome, married women were at best utilitarian, and a far cry from virgins: "We know that in a great house, there are not only vessels of gold and silver, but also of wood and earthenware," he wrote. Married women are the wood and earthenware—they propagate the species but aren't precious, "for the Church does not condemn marriage, but makes it subordinate."

Jerome argues through analogies; he takes the supremacy of the virgin for granted and then looks for startling metaphors. What his arguments lack in logic, they make up for with rhetorical flourish—he heaps image upon image, and if you don't like one, he's always ready with another. After gold, silver, and wood, he likens women to bread, barley, and dung: "It is good to feed on wheaten bread, and to eat the finest wheat flour, and yet to prevent a person pressed by hunger from devouring cow-dung, I may allow him to eat barley. Does it follow that the wheat will not have its peculiar purity, because such a one prefers barley to excrement?" The misogyny in this analogy—that married women are no better than cow dung—exemplifies the kind of haranguing bully that Jerome could be. He was capable of profound philosophy, but he was also capable of a kind of vile, histrionic vitriol that wouldn't be out of place on contemporary talk radio. Women should remain virgins, he claimed, and if you didn't agree, well, you could eat shit.

Jerome may have preferred virgins to widows, but Paula was always the exception, the one widow he preferred above all others. Even after he left Rome, she continued to follow him all over the Middle East; it was her wealth that helped fund much of his study and living expenses.

"On all sides were the seas, on all the sky," he wrote to a friend after leaving Rome. "I wandered about, uncertain where to go. Thrace, Pontus, Bithynia, the whole of Galatia and Cappadocia, Cilicia also with its burning heat—one after another shattered my energies. At last Syria presented itself to me as a most secure harbor to a shipwrecked man." Wherever he went, waiting for him, always, was faithful Paula, and together they fled into the wild. Whether or not their relationship was (as some have suggested) sexual, they kept close, hip by hip, for the rest of their lives.

When she died in 404, Jerome wrote that "if all the members of my body were to be converted into tongues, and if each of my limbs was to be gifted with a human voice, I could still do no justice to the virtues of the holy and venerable Paula."

He did his best. In a long letter to her surviving daughter, Eustochium, Jerome re-created Paula's life, not just for Eustochium but to put Paula's life in writing for all time. "Disregarding her house, her children, her servants, her property, and in a word everything connected with the world, she was eager— alone and unaccompanied (if ever it could be said that she was so)—to go to the desert made famous by its Pauls and by its Anthonies."

Jerome's depiction of Paula is part Christian saint and part epic traveler, as she wanders, Odysseus-like, toward a reunion with her true husband, Christ. Like Odysseus, she passes through Scylla and Charybdis, and upon reaching Methone

She stretched her dripping limbs upon the shore;
Then sailed past Malea and Cythera's isle,
The scattered Cyclades, and all the lands
That narrow in the seas on every side.

Allusions to the great epic wanderer Odysseus came easily to Jerome, as they have to writers from Virgil to James Joyce. Borges remarks that "throughout history, humankind has only told two stories: the story of a lost ship sailing the Mediterranean seas in quest of a beloved isle, and the story of a god who allows himself to be crucified on Golgotha." Jerome's account of Paula reads like the merging of these two books. Little of her own writing remains, so Paula is now wholly Jerome's creation: Paula the Odysseus-saint.

More than his obnoxious metaphors, it was Jerome's constant incorporation of Homer and Virgil into his writings that always bothered the orthodox—it was too self-consciously literary, too dependent on pagan sources. But even in his justification for these references, he reverts to his misogynist figures of speech, showing us once again how he views Paula. Jerome explained his use of pagan writing through a passage in Deuteronomy concerning what to do with a captive woman one wishes to marry: "Thou shalt bring her into thy house: and she shall shave her hair, and pare her nails," and after she's had a month to mourn the loss of her parents, "thou shalt go in unto her, and shalt sleep with her, and she shall be thy wife." For Jerome, this is how one deals with the pagan text: as an act of seduction, of abduction and rape. The text must be tamed. "Is it surprising," he says of the pagan text,

that I too, admiring the fairness of her form and the grace of her eloquence, desire to make that secular wisdom which is my captive and my handmaid, a matron of the true Israel? Or that shaving off and cutting away all in her that is dead whether this be idolatry, pleasure, error, or lust, I take her to myself clean and pure and beget by her servants for the Lord of Sabbath?

Domesticated, head shorn and nails pared, even the pagan source can be made to speak the truth of Christ.

No doubt, on some level, Jerome meant well. But it's difficult now to hear Paula beneath his own booming voice. She wrote a few letters that still survive, but it's not much, so it wasn't until almost a thousand years later that a very different kind of writer tried to channel Paula and dared to imagine a response to Jerome's heated rhetoric. Geoffrey Chaucer was a fairly unlikely candidate to take on Jerome, though his writings would slowly wind their way toward an epic confrontation with the great theologian.

If nothing else, Chaucer was equal to Jerome not just as a writer but also as a reader—but it's *how* he read that matters. For Chaucer, reading was an occasion not for domination but for dreaming. His early *Book of the Duchess* begins with the narrator complaining of insomnia; he picks up a book and starts to read, then falls asleep and dreams the story of the poem. *A Parliament of Fowles* is likewise born of a book-induced dream, as is *The House of Fame*. Chaucer bragged of his library, of "sixty bokes olde and newe," and self-consciously cited Virgil and Ovid, early church

writers, and French romances. But his early poems mix canonical books and dreams readily and often: If Jerome was careful
and defensive about his literary allusions, Chaucer chose chaos,
as though every book blazed some new and unorthodox path
through the mind. It was Chaucer who gave us this dream of
reading. No one before had thought of a book as such a landscape, the library as a geography. *The Inferno* opens with Dante
lost in a dark wood, but to Chaucer we owe the idea of wandering
in a book, the forest of words.

Chaucer seemed incapable of Jerome's domesticated reading—
neither of his last two works was completed. He began, could
not finish, and moved on. He did not tame the book, could not
domesticate his own story—the story outlasts him, remains wild,
uncontained. He was like a reader falling asleep before finishing
one book, who in dreaming begins the next.

After adapting *Troilus and Criseyde*, in which the fickle Criseyde abandons Troilus, breaking his heart and causing his death,
Chaucer translated the French epic *The Romance of the Rose*, famous for its misogynist monologues and portrayal of women as
bitter, conniving, duplicitous. So his next poem begins with the
god of love demanding that he atone for these "heresyes" against
love, a poem that became *The Legende of Good Women*. In a series
of repetitive narratives, Chaucer tells the stories of Cleopatra,
Thisbe, Dido, Hypsiple, Medea, Lucretia, Ariadne, Philomela,
Phyllis, and Hypermnestra. In each, an absolutely faithful woman,
a paragon of beauty and purity, is betrayed by the men in her life,

which ultimately leads to disgrace, suicide, or mutilation. Sometimes multiple calamities befall the same woman: Philomela is raped and then mutilated by her brother-in-law—her tongue cut out, she weaves a tapestry that names her assailant and then transforms into a nightingale to escape.

Chaucer wrote this in the years after he himself had been cleared of the charge of *raptus* of a woman named Cecily Champaign. The legal meaning of the word *raptus* is unclear; it usually meant "abduction" or "kidnapping." But it could also mean rape. It's not clear which of these Chaucer was accused of, or whether he was guilty. We know only that the charges were eventually dropped. Little is known about Cecily Champaign; in an age when women barely wrote, those who were not written of barely existed. She's just an entry in a legal register, a few lines in the vast corpus of human history. She became only a footnote in a grand writer's story, much as Paula was always in danger of becoming to Jerome's story.

What happened between Cecily Champaign and Chaucer? I don't know; no one does. That one legal reference is maddeningly ambiguous. It's too easy for apologists to absolve the great literary genius of culpability—after all, he was acquitted. Chaucer lived in a time when women had few rights and were victims of perpetual sexual violence, both physical and cultural. But if there is an argument to be made on Chaucer's behalf, it is in the writing itself, a writing that changed dramatically after he was acquitted of *raptus*. This was when he wrote both *The Legende of Good Women* and *The Canterbury Tales*. As one critic has suggested, it is his attempt to imagine himself in the position of a woman, and to fully imagine himself at the margins of his male-dominated society, that motivates not just his thematic concerns but "the very forms and structures of his poetry." Jerome could never really imagine a woman speaking for him—even so great a woman as Paula—but somewhere around this time, Chaucer began to try to imagine what that might be like.

After all, while twenty-two pilgrims tell their tales in Chaucer's work, there is one in particular who fascinates him: the Wife of Bath. The other pilgrims' tales celebrate saintly, pure, virginal women, but the Wife of Bath bursts into the poem, gaudy and bawdy, decrying the others' sanctimony, celebrating the carnal aspects of marriage. Her tale is that of a rapist, caught and punished, who learns that the way to happiness is in listening to women. Other characters are named by their occupation—the Knight, the Parson, the Yeoman. She is the Wife; marriage is her job. Married five times, she speaks not from "auctorite" but "experience"— and if she has an antagonist, it is the authority of church fathers like our librarian, Jerome.

Both the Wife of Bath and Chaucer deal in *textus*—he in books, she in textiles. The word means "woven," and she weaves texts into her speech, subtly upending the meanings of the writers she quotes. She reworks Jerome's metaphor of gold and wood—a household has both, she notes, and both have "doon hir lord servise." Elsewhere she recycles Jerome's ranking of white bread, barley, and cow dung, leaving the last term out and upgrading married women: Wives may be merely barley bread, but yet with the same bread "Oure Lord Jesu refresshed many a man." Like Jerome, she weaves literary references throughout her monologue, but the Wife of Bath breaks them apart, alters them—she is less a heroic Odysseus than the great weaver Penelope. Again and again, she dismantles Jerome's analogies, unknits and reweaves them.

Her prologue is long, and even after her tale is told, she doesn't shut up. While most of the other characters recede into the background, she continually interrupts, offers commentary, challenges the others. Her style is endlessly digressive—she opens up the discussions, moves further outward, interrupts others, and contradicts herself. She seems to exist to deny any kind of closure, to push the end of the text ever further away. Even in tight rhyming couplets, her thoughts drift and lose focus. She wanders, and in wandering overtakes the text, unshorn, undomesticated, untamed, and very much alive.

Jerome's story of Paula has its own digressions, but for different reasons; Jerome draws out the end of Paula's story because he cannot bear to face its conclusion. "What ails you, my soul? Why do you shudder to approach her death?" he writes. He drags himself slowly to his conclusion—"Why do I still linger, and prolong my suffering by postponing it?"—to the day in which the nuns left the convents and the hermits came in from the desert, all gathering around Paula as she died. "No weeping or lamentation followed her death," Jerome writes, because Paula was not of this world, so the death of her mortal body was nothing to weep over. He celebrates her union with Christ joyously, as he asked her to celebrate Blaesilla's death so many years earlier.

And then, in his closing lines, he slips: "I have spent the labor of two nights in dictating for you this treatise," he tells Eustochium, "and in doing so I have felt a grief as deep as your own. I say in 'dictating' for I have not been able to write it myself. As often as I have taken up my pen and have tried to fulfill my promise; my fingers have stiffened, my hand has fallen, and my power over it has vanished. The rudeness of the diction, devoid as it is of all elegance or charm, bears witness to the feeling of the writer." It is here, more so than in the rest of his writing, that Jerome becomes of this world, human. Here he ceases to be the untouchable doctor of the church and becomes a man distraught by the loss of a friend he'd known for twenty years.

A pilgrimage is the antithesis of wandering—it is all destination. But Chaucer seemed little interested in the end point. The journey to Canterbury was a convenient device for bringing together such a disparate cast of characters. He hardly mentions it in the text; in fact, the pilgrims never seem to get any closer to Canterbury.

Chaucer weaves a story of pilgrims endlessly traveling, while Jerome writes of a wanderer with purpose. He doesn't discuss Paula's trip to Phoenicia, saying, "I shall only name such places as are mentioned in the sacred books." Instead, Jerome portrays her visiting holy site after holy site; her other adventures go largely unremarked. Under Jerome's pen, all her actions are purposeful, all have meaning, all have direction, all serve Christ.

And all serve Jerome. Paula, after all, has always been a secondary saint, subordinate to Jerome in the eyes of the church. In Christian iconography, Jerome can be recognized by a skull, a book, his cardinal's attire, an owl, or a lion. Paula, by contrast, is identified chiefly by the near proximity of Jerome. A bishop of the time, Palladius, wrote of Paula that "Jerome hindered her by his jealousy, having induced her to serve his own plan." Is this true? It's hard to know. Paula is a book written by Jerome, and she is a closed book. Her hair is shaved, her nails pared: She is domesticated. All of Jerome's limbs are tongues to tell her story, but Paula herself is mute.

FOUR

Of Lament:
Radegund

It is difficult to begin the story of Saint Radegund, difficult to make sense of her life. For some time, I have turned to Euripides, particularly his plays that deal with the women of Troy after the Greeks have finally sacked the city. *Hekabe* tells the story of the Trojan queen in the days after the war, her city in ruins around her, her family decimated. Hekabe does not yet know that her last surviving son has been murdered or that her last surviving daughter is about to be offered up as a human sacrifice to the ghost of Achilles. Nevertheless, as a messenger approaches, she knows something evil is in the wind, muttering to herself:

> But something new and strange is at hand.
> Something that smells of *lament*.

Lament has a smell, a stench that precedes it. Before you know anything of Radegund, you smell it—lament and its odor precede her. The smell of unburied corpses, bleached white in the sun, of burning flesh and suppurating wounds, of the warm drink of pus and the scabs of lepers.

S aints are defined by their relationship to physical pain. There are those who bear it with humility and grace. Those who are miraculously impervious to it. Saints who relieve it in the bodies of the faithful, and saints who seek it out.

Radegund sought it out. She may have had other relationships with pain, but this one would define her. Born a Thuringian princess, Radegund was forced to marry the Frankish king Clothar; she lived with him for twenty years before he finally let her retire to a convent in Saix. Later she would found the Abbey of the Holy Cross at Poitiers. Her biographer, Venantius Fortunatus, tells us that as a child, "she would often converse with other children about her desire to be a martyr if the chance came in her time." It did not, but there were other means of self-annihilation. As an adult, she wore hair shirts and starved herself, and when this wasn't enough, Fortunatus writes, she "ordered a brass plate made, shaped in the sign of Christ. She heated it up in her cell and pressed it upon her body most deeply in two spots so that her flesh was roasted through. Thus, with her spirit flaming, she caused her very limbs to burn."

Contemporary scholars have noted that while many saints

mortified their flesh, Radegund's self-inflicted torment appears to be unique in its scope and its variety; no other saint during this time invented so many different ways to punish herself. The wounds from the brass cross not yet healed, Radegund "forced her tender limbs, already suppurating and scraped raw by the hard bristles of a hair cloth, to carry a water basin full of burning coals. Then, isolated from the rest, though her limbs were quivering, her soul was steeled for the pain. She drew it to herself, so that she might be a martyr though it was not an age of persecution."

Even her charity was conceived as a form of personal torment; when lepers came to her abbey, she disguised herself to serve them. "Not shrinking from the scurf, scabs, lice or pus, she plucked off the worms and scrubbed away the putrid flesh," Fortunatus writes. "Seizing some of the leprous women in her embrace, her heart full of love, she kissed their faces. Then, while they were seated at table, she washed their faces and hands with warm water and treated their sores with fresh unguents and fed each one."

Leprosy was thought contagious; a touch was all it took. After she had kissed the lepers, her servant asked her, "Most holy lady, when you have embraced lepers, who will kiss you?" Radegund told her, "Really, if you won't kiss me, it's no concern of mine."

In his unflinching portrayal of her unflinching torment, Fortunatus sees this as Radegund's subservience to Christ—"Thus did a woman willingly suffer such bitterness for the sweetness of Christ!" But is this only about Christ? Behind piety lie other roots of Radegund's desire for a mortal pain to rival death, the result of a life that was an endless litany of savage misery. Born in 525 to a

Thuringian king, she grew up, like Hamlet, in a household dominated by an uncle who had murdered her father and married her mother. Her uncle had a shaky truce with the Franks that he repeatedly violated, often violently, and in 531 the Frankish king Theuderic could take it no longer. He summoned his brother Clothar and pushed for war against the Thuringians. "You have every reason to be furious," he told Clothar, "both because of the injury done to me and for the slaughter of your own relations." The catalog of barbarisms attributed to the Thuringians, and so to Radegund's uncle, was long:

> They attacked our fellow-countrymen and stole their possessions. They hung our young men up to die in the trees by the muscles of their thighs. They put more than two hundred of our young women to death in the most barbarous way: they tied their arms round the necks of their horses, stampeded these animals in all directions by prodding them with goads, and so tore the girls to pieces; or else they stretched them out over the ruts of their roads, attached their arms and legs to the ground with stakes, and then drove heavily-laden carts over them again and again, until their bones were all broken and their bodies could be thrown out for the dogs and birds to feed on.

Clothar agreed, and the two brothers launched what became known as the Thuringian War against Radegund's uncle. The vengeance of the Franks was swift and complete; Gregory of Tours later described how "such a massacre of the Thuringians took place here that the bed of the river was piled high with their corpses and that the Franks crossed over them to the other side as if they were walking on a bridge." During the carnage, nearly all of Radegund's family was killed; only her young brother and she survived.

After the war came the spoils. The victorious brothers were so smitten with this child Radegund that they nearly killed one another fighting to have her. Finally they decided to gamble for her; Clothar won. In this desolation, Radegund found her new home. She was six years old.

The memories of those times would never leave her. Thirty years later, an abbess in Poitiers, she composed a long poem, "The Thuringian War," describing those savage times:

> Oh, sad state of war, malevolent destiny,
>> That fells proud kingdoms in a sudden slide.
> The roofs that stood so long in happiness are broken
>> To lie fallen beneath the vast charred ruin.
> The palace courts, where art once flourished
>> Are vaulted now with sad, glowing ashes.
> Towers artfully gilded, then shone golden-red,
>> Now drifting ashes blur the glitter to pallor.

There is nothing quite like this poem, in the medieval world or really anywhere short of the modern age. Euripedes may have written about the Trojan women, but nowhere else have I ever heard of such an ancient firsthand account of war from the perspective of defeated women. Women who had not even the comfort that the heroes of Troy had, who could not go to heroic death like Hektor. Women who saw that before them lay only slavery and rape.

Slavery and rape lay in store for Radegund, though her husband, Clothar, had the decency to wait until she was in her early teens before consummating their marriage. When Hekabe says, "I am dead before death, from pressure of evil," it is Radegund who comes to my mind. Fortunatus tells us how at night,

> when she lay with her prince she would ask leave to rise and leave the chamber to relieve nature. Then she would prostrate herself in prayer under a hair cloak by the privy so long that the cold pierced her through and through and only her spirit was warm. Her whole flesh prematurely dead, indifferent to her body's torment, she kept her mind intent on Paradise and counted her suffering trivial.

After Clothar murdered her last surviving brother in 550, she begged him to let her go; finally he allowed her to retire to a villa in Saix. There she lived in relative peace, burning her flesh and tending to lepers and never for a moment forgetting what she had seen and lived through, the pain of her memories only barely replaced by the physical pain of loving Christ. In 558, Clothar was nearing the end of his life and sent for Radegund; he was, according to her second biographer, "grieving over the grave loss he had suffered in letting so great and good a queen leave his side and that within himself he had no wish to live unless he could get her back again." But Radegund by then understood that her spiritual husband was preferable to her earthly one: According to legend, as Clothar came searching, Radegund fled to an oat field where the grain miraculously grew suddenly high around her, hiding her from view.

Reality was a bit more mundane; Radegund had likely recognized that, after a lifetime of bloody deeds, Clothar was looking for absolution through charitable works. And she was shrewd enough to extort money from him to found the abbey and guarantee that she would be left in peace.

She desired only to be left in peace and to be out of sight. Once, when lepers came to the abbey, "she laid a table with dishes, spoons, little knives, cups and goblets, and wine and she went in herself secretly that none might see her." After the coals burned her so deeply that her arms bled, she covered the wounds lest anyone notice: "Silently, she concealed the holes, but the putrefying blood betrayed the pain that her voice did not reveal." She wanted invisibility, but her miracles and her biographers made this impossible, and her quiet piety was made plain for all to see. As Fortunatus put it, "What she did secretly was to become known to all people."

Fortunatus and those who came later wanted to make a symbol of her, a visible image of the blessings of Christ's love. A beacon of faith in a turbulent world, burning for all to see. But it is not clear at all that this was something she wanted for herself. She wanted to be left alone with her sisters at Poitiers.

In the Abbey of the Holy Cross at Poitiers, she wrote "The Thuringian War," recounting the miseries of her life, at the poem's heart a plea to her last remaining kinsman, Adelmarth, a cousin who had not responded to her repeated letters. And it was here in the abbey of Poitiers, that many of Radegund's miracles occurred as she brought health and remedy to those around her. Among the stories recounted by Fortunatus is that of the nun Aminia, who "suffered so with dropsical swelling that she seemed to have reached her end." As the sisters waited for her death, Aminia had a vision in which

it seemed to her that the most venerable blessed Radegund ordered her to descend nude into a bath with no water in it. Then, with her own hand, the blessed one seemed to pour oil on the sick woman's head and cover her with a new garment. After this strange ritual, when she awakened from her sleep, all trace of the disease had disappeared. She had not even sweated it away for the water was consumed from within. As a result of this new miracle, no vestige of disease was left in her belly.

This is the arc of Radegund's life: from the endurance of pain to the miraculous cessation of the pain of others, her self-inflicted pain an axis around which the other two poles tilt. This is the touch of Radegund's hand, a touch that brings peace to others even as it does violence to herself.

Radegund describes herself in her poem as "I, the barbarian woman." To the Franks, the Thuringians were indeed barbarians—the word derived from the Greek, meaning simply "anyone not Greek." It is onomatopoeic, the *bar bar* meant to invoke the gibberish of the foreign tongue. To be a barbarian is to have only gibberish for language, to speak without sense.

There is no gibberish in Radegund's words, but there is a wordless wail of grief that rends its way through her poetry:

> Nor could the captive press a kiss on the threshold
>> Nor cast one backward glance toward what was lost.
> A wife's naked feet trod in her husband's blood
>> And the tender sister stepped over the fallen brother.
> The boy torn from his mother's embrace, his funeral plaint
>> Hung on her lips, with all her tears unshed.
> So to lose the life of a child is not the heaviest lot,
>> Gasping, the mother lost even her pious tears.

Radegund's poetic technique is to layer image upon image; a horror is borne first by captives, then by wives and husbands, then by sisters and brothers, then by mothers, children. Each grief named in turn, all gathered up by her lone remaining voice until the words themselves buckle and break under her repetition, and lament—pure lament—spills forth:

> I, the barbarian woman, seek not to count these tears,
> Nor to keep afloat in the melancholy lake of all
>   those drops.
> Each one had her own tears; I alone have them all,
>   Anguish is private and public both to me.
> Fate was kind to those whom the enemy struck down.
>   I, the sole survivor, must weep for them all.
> Not only must I mourn the near ones who died:
>   I also grieve for those still blessed with life.
> My face often moistened, my eyes are blurred,
>   My murmurs are secret but my care unstilled.

Unstilled cares finally broke Hekabe, turning her wailing, according to legend, into the bark of a dog. Her human voice, no longer able to contain all that misery, went beyond gibberish and senselessness into the nonhuman. Radegund wrote poetry because she could not send a wordless wail to Adelmarth, because she could not call him to her with the barking of a dog.

She was still living with Clothar when he had her brother murdered, and Radegund could do nothing but sit in mute silence as the reports of her husband's brutality came in. Her brother's death went unmourned, as had those of the hundreds of Thuringians killed decades earlier. Fortunatus saw this as a good thing because it was this outrage that finally broke their marriage and allowed Radegund to retire to Saix, where her sainted life could begin: "If divinity fosters it," he tells us, "misfortune often leads to salvation. Thus her innocent brother was murdered so that she might come to live in religion." But if Fortunatus could gloss over this horror, Radegund could not.

> The youth was struck down while in his first downy beard,
> Nor did I, his absent sister, attend the dire funeral.
> I lost him and could not even close his pious eyes
> Nor lie across the corpse in final farewell,
> My hot tears could not warm his freezing bowels.
> I placed no kiss upon his dying flesh,
> No embrace in my misery. I could not hang weeping on
> his neck
> Nor sighing, warm the unlucky corpse in my bosom.

In this, too, Radegund is barbaric, one mark of the barbarian being a lack of proper reverence for the dead—this being a thing that separates the barbarians from those excellent Greeks. In Euripides' play, Odysseus tells Hekabe,

> You barbarians don't know how to treat your friends as
> friends,
> how to venerate men who die beautiful deaths.

Maybe so, but barbarism is always relative: Odysseus has just told Hekabe that her last remaining daughter is to be sacrificed to the ghost of Achilles, the man who dragged the corpse of her son Hektor through the dirt. Hekabe—who once saved Odysseus's life—now strikes him as barbaric for not honoring the world-killer Achilles with her daughter and with the gratitude for the existence of heroic men like him.

Perhaps barbarism is only this wordless, mute wail of the defeated, of women who cannot even mourn their kindred dead. A lament without end that strikes the ears of victorious brutes as pure gibberish, like the sound of a barking dog.

At its heart, "The Thuringian War" is just this: a plea to one of her last surviving kin, a longing for contact, for a word of friendship in a life of pain and death. Radegund lived in a time without pity, a time when the only refuge for a woman without means was to be found in religion. Radegund, a princess who lost everything, turned to Christ for solace. But for Fortunatus to say that her masochism came from religious fervor and not from the desolation of her life and the annihilation of her family may not be entirely accurate. Bound within the walls of the convent, Radegund thinks not of Christ but of her cousin:

> If the monastery's sacred cloister did not keep me back,
>   I'd come unheralded to the region where you bide.
> Swift would I pass by ship through tempest-tossed waves
>   Racing gladly through the gales of wintry water.
> For love of you, would I press more strongly through
>   the shifting tides;
> What sailors dread would never make me quake.

If the wave broke the keel in the perilous waters,

    I would still seek you rowing on the surface of the sea.

If by unlucky chance, the planks refused to bear me,

    I would come to you exhausted from swimming.

At sight of you, I would deny the journey's perils

    For that would sweetly take the sorrow from the wreck

Yes, if fate had ripped from me at last my doleful life,

    I would have you bear me to a sandy tomb.

I would come to you a sightless corpse if your pious eyes

    Would turn at last to carry out my funeral rites.

Surely you, who spurn my living tears, would weep at

      my burial.

    Surely you, who deny me a word now, would mourn.

In the two hundred lines of the poem, Radegund barely mentions Christ. Instead she recalls in graphic detail horrors forty years old and makes a desperate plea for a word from a beloved cousin. Reading it alongside Fortunatus's biography is jarring; he makes almost no mention of her suffering except as opportunities to enrich her faith and her love of Christ. Radegund lived in a time when only two kinds of suffering were worth noting: the blessed suffering of Christ or the senseless suffering of the barbarian. Between these worlds, Radegund crafts a poem that mentions Christ and barbarians but is about neither, a poem that is a lament so pure that it has a physical presence, a body and a smell of its own.

    Radegund eventually got her wish and has gradually faded

from sight. There are still churches dedicated to her, but she has little of the cult following she once had. The convent dedicated to her in Cambridge became Jesus College, Cambridge, and while she remains its patron saint, the nearby street Radegund Lane was long ago renamed Jesus Lane. The oat fields have once again grown up around her, and she has disappeared again from searching eyes. But the smell of that lament still remains, an echo on the high breeze.

FIVE

Quixote's Madness:
Teresa of Avila

Lost in the limitless labyrinth of books is Teresa. Born in March 1515 in Avila, she was born for reading and as a young girl read incessantly: "I do not believe I was ever happy if I had not a new book," she writes in the opening of her autobiography. She learned this love from her mother, who was fond of chivalric romances and always made time for her children to read. Teresa's father disapproved, thought it a waste of time, a corrupting of his children's minds. Teresa and her siblings had to keep the reading a secret—she began to call it "an addiction," her "little fault." She read in the quiet of dark spaces, much like the young Marcel Proust, who centuries later described seeking out the "dim coolness" of his room to evade his family and read in secret.

In the lives of the saints, she found an early love of martyrdom, and when she was seven, she and her brother ran away from home to be martyred at the hands of the Moors, only to be returned home by her uncle. Perhaps her father was right: Reading was dangerous, at least for someone like Teresa, under the thrall of her emotions; a love of books went hand in hand with a love of death.

At the time, Teresa found no fault with her reading: "It did not seem wicked to me," she wrote many years later in her autobiography, "to waste many hours of the day and the night on this vain occupation, even though I had to keep it secret from my father." Even as an adult writing of those times, she saw in retrospect the vices of reading, how it "began to chill my desires and lead me astray in other respects as well."

What to make of a book that begins with the perils of reading? Should we put it down, go no further? To keep reading, it seems, is to implicate ourselves—it is our little fault that drives us on, our vain occupation, our addiction. We may read, but to read Teresa's autobiography is already to be an interloper, to trespass into a world you've been warned against. She doesn't want us here, even as she beckons us to come in. Teresa's is a strange book, a book with no place for a reader.

Her mother died when Teresa was twelve, and Teresa fell even further under the sway of her romances. When she was fifteen, her father placed her in a convent. There she found her calling, despite being plagued in her early years by serious health problems. Under the direction of a Franciscan, Peter of Alcantara, she set out in 1560 to found a Carmelite convent in Avila. Her convent brought back the old order, reinstating flagellation and discalcation (the forbidding of the wearing of shoes), and from 1567 to 1576, Teresa set up convents of discalced Carmelites throughout Spain.

Around the same time, she was asked by her confessor, Pedro Ibáñez, to record the events of her conversion, a record that became her autobiography. In the centuries since, it has become the most widely read book in Spanish after *Don Quixote*, which first appeared only thirty-five years after Teresa wrote her autobiography. Like Cervantes's masterpiece, Teresa's autobiography is about the dangers of reading. Cervantes's Quixote is poisoned by the same chivalric romances that Teresa read as a child. He sells his estate to buy more and more books until they finally drive him mad and he begins a quest not unlike that attempted by Teresa when she was seven.

Teresa's story caught like wildfire. It may have been about the dangers of reading, written for a private audience, but that hasn't stopped the thousands who have flocked to it. After all, we *want* to eavesdrop. We *want* to read what is forbidden in the dim coolness of private rooms. We want to be affected by the wickedness of the book, to share in Teresa's little addiction, to succumb to Quixote's madness.

~🦋~

Teresa's life is proof that she finally triumphed over this vice, reformed her ways, and followed Christ. But traces of her love of reading remain all over her autobiography. In a book that opens with a scene of reading, she recalls with bitterness how her confessor removed all the books in Spanish from the convent— "I felt it deeply because some of them gave me recreation and I could not go on reading them, since now I only had them in Latin." Later she calls Christ Himself "a veritable book in which I have read the truth." Hers may be a story about God, but it is told as an allegory of the reader and the writer.

Her writing is often chaotic; she asks permission before speaking, she loses herself on tangents before returning to a half-remembered topic, and she's at times repetitive. "I seem to have wandered from my subject," she says more than a few times. At times she supplicates herself abjectly before her confessor; at other times she reprimands him for a dim understanding of Christ. Through all this, she seems to acknowledge that the book will have no editor and that she will never look back on what she's written. And she's not bothered by this. Like that of a nineteenth-century spirit medium, Teresa's is an automatic writing.

We have long since lost the ability to see the art in this; in the twenty-first century, we are too used to the idea that the work of art must have a holistic and unified effect, that it must be perfect. Even contemporary writers who might emulate such chaos—

Nabokov in *Pale Fire*, for example—do so deliberately, with extreme calculation. The better corollary to Teresa would be writers like Gerard de Nerval and Antonin Artaud. Like Artaud's works, Teresa's autobiography comes alive in its madness, though *madness* is not the right word for many of these writers. *Ecstatic* is better—writing that doesn't tell a story or impress an idea so much as it records the simple alchemy of putting pen to paper.

Ultimately Teresa's autobiography is a book about the act of writing itself. "I see so much perdition in this world," she writes, "that even if my writing has no other effect than to weary this hand that wields the pen, it brings me some comfort." Teresa's autobiography is a strange mixture in which she writes of the dangers of reading and the pleasures of writing. Like Gregory's or Radegund's, Teresa's work comes alive when it breaks against itself, when its sutures rupture and break, when something unintended shows through.

This kind of writing is always vulnerable, and readers and commentators always want to reduce it to something it's not. The danger is in making her sane, in reading the work as a holistic piece of art. The error would be to read it as complete, a masterpiece; doing so, as many have, is to read her ecstasy in the most banal of ways.

Many of us outside of Spain know her through Bernini's famous sculpture—her head thrown back, mouth agape, eyes closed, as a cherub hovers above her with an arrow. Bernini's sculpture depicts perhaps the most famous moment in Teresa's autobiography, a description of an ecstatic vision that comes late in the book:

> In his hands I saw a great golden spear, and at the iron tip there appeared to be a point of fire. This he plunged into my heart several times so that it penetrated to my entrails. When he pulled it out, I felt that he took them with it, and left me utterly consumed by the great love of God. The pain was so severe that it made me utter several moans. The sweetness caused by this intense pain is so extreme that one cannot possibly wish it to cease, nor is one's soul then content with anything but God. This is not a physical pain, but a spiritual pain, though the body has some share in it—even a considerable share.

Whatever was happening in Teresa's mind and in her body as this experience was taking place, most modern commentators have seen only one possible explanation. Marie Bonaparte—a practicing psychoanalyst and a friend of Freud who was at the time measuring the distance between the clitoris and vagina in 250 women—spoke for many readers when she declared, unequivocally, that Teresa's revelation was nothing more than a "violent venereal orgasm."

Bonaparte was something of a literalist, to be sure, but she makes plain the problem, the danger in reading Teresa. To read

FIGURE 3: *The Ecstasy of Saint Teresa* (1647–1652),
Giovanni Lorenzo Bernini SANTA MARIA DELLA VITTORIA,
ROME, ITALY/ALINARI/THE BRIDGEMAN ART LIBRARY

her and see only sex, as we have been conditioned to do, is the same error as reading her and ignoring sexuality altogether.

One understands why Teresa tells us how she "earnestly begged the Lord to grant me no more favors if they must have outward and visible signs." To see a saint in rapture is to misunderstand, and to read her ecstasy is to misread. Perhaps there was some divine accession to her request when she died in October 1582, just as Catholic countries were switching from the Julian calendar to the Gregorian calendar, a realignment that necessitated the loss of October 5–14. Thus, she left this earth sometime between the night of October 4 and the morning of October 15, in those strange, invisible days of history.

Bernini's genius is in the massive cloak that covers Teresa so that only her face and hands are visible. Everything else lies below the surface, lost in those endless folds. In there somewhere is the ecstasy of writing, the relationship of reader and writer. You may guess at its contours, but you will never know its shape. It is under the folds of such a cloak that the perfect book, and the perfect library, lie. Hidden, shapeless, but somehow moving, somehow alive.

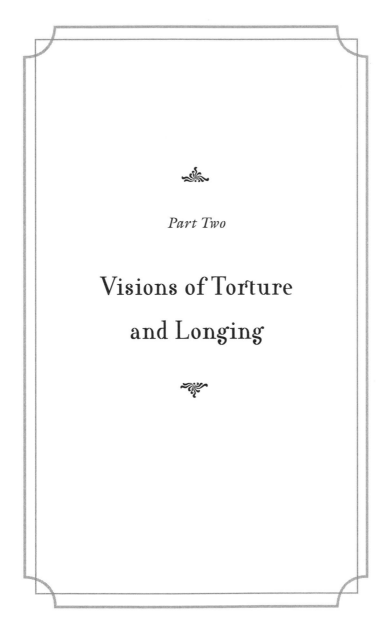

Part Two

Visions of Torture
and Longing

SIX

Trickster Laughs:
Lawrence of the Gridirons

B ack in Jesuit high school, every day in chemistry, our teacher would begin class with a reading of the day's saint. He had a small book of feast days that he kept in his breast pocket—one of those cheap, staple-bound books you used to be able to buy in grocery-store checkout lines—and would read in his stilted Texas accent of the martyrs and persecutions of the early church.

To this day, I remember his voice quite clearly, but from a year of feast days, the only saint I remember is Lawrence. A deacon under Pope Sixtus II in the third century, Lawrence was martyred during the Roman emperor Valerian's persecutions in 258 and, according to legend, was executed on a gridiron over an open flame.

As he was being burned alive, so the story goes, he cried out to his tormentors, "This side's done; turn me over and have a bite."

At this, the whole class burst into laughter, and I remember our teacher's grim face as he looked up at us, quietly apoplectic at our sacrilege, and said drily, "You don't laugh at that. We're talking about a man dying here. That's not funny."

But of course, it *is* funny. It's not for nothing that Lawrence is recognized now as the patron saint of comedians. Lawrence is the trickster saint, the buffoon, the clown. After Pope Sixtus was executed, Valerian demanded that Lawrence turn over the treasury of the church; Lawrence instead gave away all of the church's property and then brought Valerian a group of blind, crippled, and homeless men, telling the Roman emperor that these were the *true* treasures of the Church. Sure, this isn't laugh-out-loud funny, but still.

My chemistry teacher snapped at us because he, like so many believers, conflated the sacred and the solemn. Patriarchal religions like Christianity tend to be like this. The French philosopher and atheist Georges Bataille points out that no one ever laughs in the Gospels—the good news may be joyous, but it's not funny.

But in other religions, laughter is integral. The anthropologist Byrd Gibbens writes, "Many native traditions held clowns and tricksters as essential to any contact with the sacred. People could not pray until they had laughed, because laughter opens and frees from rigid preconception. Humans had to have tricksters within the most sacred ceremonies for fear that they forget the sacred comes through upset, reversal, surprise. The trickster in most native traditions is essential to creation, to birth."

Because of this, Lawrence seems to me a saint imported from another religion, closer to Coyote or Raven than to Stephen or Catherine. At the moment of his death is this sudden reversal; with one joke, he takes the power back from his torturers, and the moment breaks open. In our laughter, we understand a little more about life and death. Georges Bataille also writes that uncontrolled laughter brings us to the edge of an abyss, a "stage of rupture, of letting go of things." And if Bataille reminds us that behind laughter lies death, Lawrence reminds us that to go willingly to your own execution is to laugh at death, and to laugh at death is also to laugh.

Like most martyrs, Lawrence has multiple patronages. He protects not just comedians but also students as well as Rome and Rotterdam, Canada and Sri Lanka. Perhaps most bizarre, perhaps even disturbing: He is the patron saint of barbecues.

In Christian iconography, saints are usually depicted with the instruments of their torture, as with Catherine and her wheel or Sebastian impaled by arrows. And so Lawrence is often seen holding a grill, sometimes balanced on his shoulder, the instrument of his death used to distinguish images of him from the other martyrs.

But over the centuries, this grill has gone from being Lawrence's mode of death to his primary hobby: There's Lawrence, the guy with the grill, always up for a backyard get-together, always there to bless your Super Bowl party.

How does this happen? How do torture and recreation get so casually commingled? It turns out to be somewhat common among Christian martyrs, and Lawrence is not the only saint who's suffered such a bizarre distortion. Agatha's torture included having her breasts cut off, and she is commonly depicted as holding those breasts on a tray before her. But the laity didn't always recognize these tan lumps as breasts. They were misread often enough both as bells and as loaves of bread that she has become the patron saint of bell-forgers and bakers. And then there's Bartholomew, flayed alive, who holds, in addition to his own skin, the tool used to cut that skin off, a tool that looks sort of like a cheese cutter, so Florentine cheese merchants took Bartholomew as their patron.

These corruptions happen from the bottom up, from the uneducated and working classes, adrift in a world of subsistence and hardship, searching for patrons to aid them. In search of solace, they find these bizarre images of disembodied torture and do their best to make sense of them.

It's not that the image of Lawrence with the gridiron doesn't tell a story, but you have to already know that story in order to recognize it. Seeing a painting of an otherwise healthy-looking man holding a grill means nothing without some context.

The image of the saint works like a parable: It doesn't tell a story so much as hide it. When asked about the parables by his disciples, Jesus tells them bluntly, "The knowledge of the secrets of the kingdom of heaven has been given to you, but not to them," meaning the unbelievers. He goes on, "Whoever has will be given more, and he will have an abundance. Whoever does not have, even what he has will be taken from him. This is why I speak to them in parables: Though looking, they do not see; though hearing, they do not understand."

Or, as Kafka put it, "all these parables really set out to say merely that the incomprehensible is incomprehensible, and we know that already."

The image of Lawrence and his gridiron is a parable in the sense that only the self-selecting few who already know his story recognize it in such an incomprehensible image. It is those who don't know the story of Lawrence who misread it as barbecue rather than torture, doing their best to make sense of a visual parable. They look but do not see.

It is perhaps because of this inherent ambiguity that images were always distrusted in the early church. Inheriting a legacy of the Hebraic tradition and its second commandment forbidding graven images, early Christians thought pictures inherently untrustworthy, lacking the rock-solid truth of words, and banned them accordingly.

It wasn't until 600, several hundred years after Lawrence's death, that this changed with Serenius the Iconoclast (literally, "breaker of images"). The bishop of Marseilles, Serenius, had found his recently converted flock making images of Jesus, and he destroyed them. When Pope Gregory the Great got word of this, he sent a long letter praising Serenius's zeal but telling him to leave the images alone since "those who do not know letters may at least read by seeing on the walls what they are unable to read in books." With that stroke, a centuries-old ban on image-making was ended, and the floodgates opened.

For Gregory, images are books for the illiterate, but if so, they are a curious kind of book, one whose meaning is strangely open to interpretation, in which the poor and the illiterate have been free to adapt the ambiguous images adorning churches in whatever manner might give them solace or hope. It is here, in these misinterpretations, in the odd patronages of the saints, that Catholicism reveals its folk aspect, its native traditions and local customs. And it is here that Saint Lawrence reigns, his trickster laughter stretching the world beyond the humorlessness of the gospel truth and fundamentalism. On the other side of orthodoxy lies this legacy of distortion and expansion, where we look and do not see, yet see something new, something else entirely.

SEVEN.

Anatomical Annihilations: Bartholomew

I can think of no saint whose torture was more dramatic than Bartholomew's. I'll never forget the first time I saw Marco d'Agrate's sculpture of him in the Milan cathedral; from a distance, he looked like some emaciated, bald hermit wrapped in a sash. Only when I got close did I see that he wasn't emaciated: That was his bare muscle I was looking at. What I had thought was a sash was in fact his own skin, peeled off his body and draped around his shoulders.

Bartholomew was one of the twelve apostles, but in the Gospels, he has none of the importance of Peter, Thomas, or Judas Iscariot. Somewhat on the fringe, he seems to be there mostly to round out the twelve. It's not until after Jesus's death that Bartholomew's story begins to take on life. After the events of the New Testament, according to most accounts, Bartholomew traveled to India to spread the gospel. There he converted the king, Polimius, by healing him from an incurable disease, though whatever goodwill he may have engendered was quickly squandered when he began destroying the various pagan statues in the palace. Under pressure from incensed priests, the king's brother responded to Bartholomew's disruption first by crucifying him upside down, then by flaying him alive, and finally by beheading him. Among these tortures, it is the flaying that became the mode of punishment iconically associated with Bartholomew. Thus, popular depictions of the saint show him carrying his own skin—often he holds his flayed skin toward the viewer, as if presenting a gift.

The question is: What kind of gift is this? And what are we to make of such a thing? His body opened and displayed like no one else's—muscle, vein, and organ visible—Bartholomew offers us the gift of the body in a unique way and thereby presents us with the secret knowledge of the body's inner workings.

In the fifteenth century, very little was known about the way the body worked. Dissections were done only a few times a year because the human body was doubly problematic, paradoxically both sacred and defiling. Religious and secular authorities would allow dissections only under extremely rare conditions and specifically ritualistic circumstances. The men who actually carried out dissections in that era were called *sectors*, and they were not doctors—they were barbers, laborers. Doctors and professors did not handle the corpse because in addition to being sacred, it was also taboo; the unburied body still carried with it a ritual pollution. So while it had a pedagogic value, the aristocratic doctors and lecturers weren't going to touch it; they left the actual dissection to lower-class tradesmen. Standing beside the sector would be the *ostensor*, a junior faculty member, and it was his job to narrate the dissection to the assembled students. Above them all, a senior faculty member, the *lector*, would read from an anatomy textbook in Latin. It was the ostensor's job to translate between the lector and the sector, to translate from the Latin into the vernacular, and to translate the corpus of learning into the corpse.

It was a system designed to foster ignorance. Of all the various roles involved, that of the lector with his book was the most important—students were in class to learn what had been written down centuries ago, and the body itself merely illustrated what the text said. The text in question came from Galen, the third-century father of anatomy, who never dissected a human body himself. Instead, he developed his ideas through two different methods: He palpated and observed the outer workings of his patients, and then he dissected other animals that he imagined correlated well with humans, particularly apes and dogs. From these two data points, he did his best to infer how human anatomy functioned. But the interior of the body itself remained out of sight to Galen as well as to the countless doctors who took his ideas as gospel in the 1,300 years that followed.

All this changed with Andreas Vesalius, who revolutionized

modern anatomy. In 1537, he was given the chair of surgery and anatomy at the University of Padua, and though he had studied Galen, he opted not to take his work as unassailable truth. Instead, he dispensed with both the lector and the sector and performed the dissections himself, narrating what he saw to his pupils. With the help of a sympathetic judge who made more bodies available to him, Vesalius upended the Galenic regime of medicine and introduced a thoroughly new and completely empirical description of the human body. With the 1543 publication of his opus, *De Humani Corporis Fabrica*, Vesalius reinvented anatomy.

Marco d'Agrate's striking sculpture of Bartholomew appeared in 1562, only twenty years after Vesalius's textbook. This hardly strikes me as a coincidence; there was a newfound interest in the skinless saint because of Vesalius, particularly because of a common image that appeared in *De Humani Corporis Fabrica* and a number of other textbooks that followed. Vesalius got rid of lector, ostensor, and sector in favor of one anatomist, and the artists who illustrated these medical texts took this process one step further, removing Vesalius altogether. What begins to appear is the corpse alone—removed from the anatomy theater, the corpse now offers itself. It is its own dissector.

This is the *ecorché*, its name from the French verb "to flay." The skinned body of the ecorché appears in early editions of *De Humani Corporis Fabrica* and becomes increasingly common in anatomical textbooks throughout the Renaissance. It has moved off the operating table and into a fictional countryside, sometimes appearing amid classical ruins. Often it appears actively participating in its own mutilation, either holding the knife that cut its skin away or physically peeling back its skin with its hands or teeth.

One inspiration for this image was the story of the satyr Marsyas, from Ovid's *Metamorphoses*, a story that would have been familiar to most Renaissance artists. Marsyas found a cursed set of pipes and learned to play them—arrogantly, he challenged Apollo to a musical contest. Apollo, of course, won and chose as his punishment to skin Marsyas alive:

> "Help!" Marsyas clamored. "Why are you stripping me from myself? Never again, I promise! Playing the pipe is not worth this!" But in spite of his cries his skin was torn of the whole surface of his body: it was all one raw wound. Blood flowed everywhere, his nerves were exposed, unprotected, his veins pulsed with no skin to cover them. It was possible to count his throbbing organs, and the chambers of his lungs, clearly visible within his breast.

Ovid emphasizes the particularly visible aspect of this ghastly punishment—one can count organs and chambers that are "clearly visible." But what he describes is also fundamentally unrepresentable. He speaks of Marsyas being "all one raw wound," and a wound, like a void, does not exist unto itself. The ecorché is a sort of visual paradox, an explicitly visual form of that which cannot be

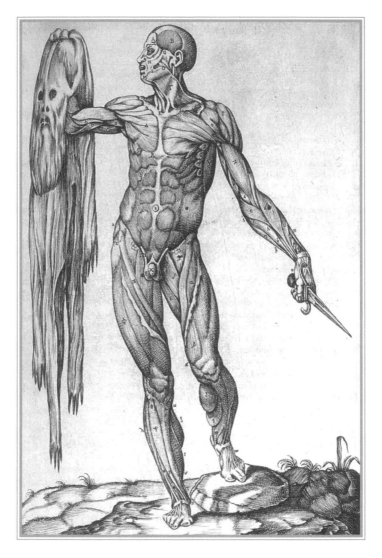

FIGURE 4: *Flayed Man Holding a Dagger and His Skin* from
Juan Valverde de Amusco's *Antomia del Corp Humano* (1560),
artist unknown

seen. So Marsyas became something of a popular artistic challenge—how does one paint that which has no shape, no container, no outline? We have gone from the body being invisible, to the very limits of what's possible of representation—the ecorché, standing relaxed, and by no means in any visible pain, no hint of scream or cry on the face of this mutilated body. If anatomists like Vesalius sought to reveal what had always been invisible, artists who now illustrated these textbooks sought to make visible what was logistically and visually impossible.

Cadavers available for dissection were first and foremost the bodies of executed criminals. Since burial in consecrated ground was necessary for one's resurrection, certainly no one was going to donate her or his body to science. Dissection itself was a kind of second punishment, another way of condemning the criminal, and as with the case of Marsyas, flayed by a god, flaying acted as a particularly visible form of damnation. In England, the so-called Murder Act of 1752 attempted to stop a rise in violent crime by mandating that all executed criminals, after death, would either be strung up in gibbets or dissected in the medical schools. Without proper burial, these criminals had no chance of salvation. Execution took away your life; dissection took away your soul.

In addition, these corpses were not just dismembered—they were flayed. Flaying, historians have suggested, was rather uncommon, but when it was used, it had a specific symbolic reference. The ecorché loses all identity; neither the skinned body nor the skin itself preserve anything of the image of the punished; flayed, the condemned's identity is ultimately obliterated, and the condemned ceases to be human. Flaying, according to one historian, was used "not merely a means of inflicting a cruel death on a criminal, but of marking abhorrence of breaches of the fundamental bond of human society."

The fact is that the skin itself was often the very means of demarcating one's punishment. In Kafka's "In the Penal Colony," the execution device works by inscribing the crime of the condemned onto his skin over and over again until he dies—the skin being the ledger on which the machine indicates why this individual is being excised from humanity.

The historical precedent for Kafka's idea can be found in the practice of anthropodermic bibliopegy, that is, binding books with human skin. Often this was done as a nonpunitive measure, but in early-nineteenth-century England, it became particularly popular as a means of marking the extreme status of the criminal. In 1827, a man named William Corder murdered his girlfriend in a barn (the so-called Red Barn Murder); caught and convicted, he was sentenced not only to death but to dissection at Cambridge University afterward. And after the dissection, one of the attending surgeons removed a portion of Corder's skin, tanned it, and used it as the cover of a book containing the court record of his trial. The body of William Burke, the famous murderer who sold his victims to medical schools, underwent a similar process. After his dissection, part of his skin was made into a wallet that was given to the doorkeeper of the dissection lab; another part was used to bind a book containing a record of Burke's crimes that was given to Sir Walter Scott.

Flaying is the ultimate punishment, the one that removes you from human society, literally and symbolically, in a way perhaps no other torture can match. The ecorché is on the very outside limit of society and representation, well beyond the bounds of the human.

But there is a difference between the corpse laid out on the table under Vesalius's inquisitive eyes and the ecorché who holds up his own skin to show us the interior; now the condemned is actively involved in this dissection. Having been killed, damned, and obliterated, the figure still offers itself to us. Why?

Some have argued that it was extremely important that the cadavers be made to participate actively in their own mutilation— even though these were the bodies of criminals, there was still a great deal of anxiety on the part of the medical community about such a complete annihilation of a fellow human's soul. We should note that although these were executed criminals, they were not all murderers; the majority of cadavers dissected in sixteenth-century Italy had been executed for lesser crimes, including theft and sodomy. Such a harsh punishment for minor crimes may not have set well with everyone involved, so depicting the dissected bodies in a such a peaceful, even helpful, pose, as though they were giving their consent to the practice, helped alleviate these fears and legitimize dissection.

So this is the gift of Bartholomew, the gift of visibility, a secret knowledge of the body's workings, even at the cost of his own annihilation.

Intentionally or not, the images of the ecorché that appear in anatomy textbooks repeatedly evoke Bartholomew; specifically, they call to mind what remains a central image of Bartholomew, one found in Michelangelo's *Last Judgment* in the Sistine Chapel.

Michelangelo undertook this massive fresco, painted between 1537 and 1541, just as Vesalius was beginning his revolution in nearby Padua. It was immediately controversial because Michelangelo had brought genitals into the space of the church, depicting them explicitly on many of the figures. Making visible that which should remain hidden is always going to catch the eye of the censor, but in addition, critics singled out his depiction of Bartholomew, who stands holding his flayed skin just to the lower right of Christ. To put something so horrific at the center of such a majestic painting, many felt, was beyond the pale. "It is necessarily crude and wanton," the censor Johannes Molanus wrote in 1570, "to depict Saint Bartholomew totally flayed like a monster of old." More important than this breach of decorum, though, was a central contradiction—Bartholomew does not appear to be holding his own skin. Don Miniato wrote to Vasari in 1545, "There are a thousand heresies here, and above all the beardless skin of Saint Bartholomew, while the skinned one has a long beard, which shows that the skin is not his."

FIGURE 5: *Detail from The Last Judgment* (1537–1541), the
Sistine Chapel, Michelangelo Buonarroti VATICAN MUSEUMS AND
GALLERIES, VATICAN CITY, ITALY/THE BRIDGEMAN ART LIBRARY

It wasn't until 1925 that this mystery was finally resolved when a physician named Francesco de Cava realized that Bartholomew is not holding his own skin—he's holding Michelangelo's. What we're looking at is a self-portrait, the artist as a flayed pelt of human skin. It is, in fact, the only known self-portrait of Michelangelo.

Why did he place his only known likeness here, in this most gothic of places? Leo Steinberg points out that Michelangelo did not believe that everyone would be saved in the resurrection. As a result, he expressed a certain amount of anxiety about his own salvation. And so, Steinberg argues, this painting, for all its universal themes, hides a personal drama. Drawing a diagonal through the painting—what Steinberg calls the "line of fate"—connects God in the upper left corner to Satan in the lower right, and the line bisects, almost exactly, the face of Michelangelo in the skin Bartholomew is holding. Michelangelo would have known, Steinberg argues, the passage from the Book of Job: "I know that my Redeemer liveth, and in the last day I shall rise out of the earth. And I shall be clothed again with my skin, and in my flesh I shall see my God. This hope is laid up in my bosom." These lines were inscribed on Bertoldo di Giovanni's medal for a bishop in the Medici family, which Michelangelo would have been familiar with, a medal that also featured an abbreviated scene of *The Last Judgment*. The skin is something of a figure for the as yet unredeemed sinner, the remains of the mortal body that have not yet been reanimated by God's grace.

In other words, Bartholomew holds not his own skin but that of Michelangelo, the painter who hangs midway between God and Satan, whose fate is not yet determined. The work of the apocalypse almost done, Bartholomew intercedes on behalf of the painter, offering up his as yet unredeemed skin to Jesus, plaintively asking the Savior to animate it once more with Michelangelo's soul.

The Last Judgment, finished two years before Vesalius's textbook, would have been well known by many of the artists illustrating anatomical textbooks. In these textbooks, the ecorché appears serene, complicit in his mutilation. And this may be because of the anatomists' anxiety over what they were doing, an attempt to reassure them of the importance of dissection. But like Marsyas, the cadaver is cursed by God, and like Marsyas, the punishment may not fit the crime. And so, like Michelangelo, the cadaver is desperate for absolution. In holding its skin up for inspection, it echoes Bartholomew pleading on behalf of the painter, and in that echo we are once again reminded of the horrific acts of execution, dismemberment, and finally obliteration of the dissected corpse. At the limits of the human, it is Bartholomew, the flayed one, who speaks for the criminals and the artists, who offers up his own skin to save ours, who tries to bring these dead back into the fold.

EIGHT

The Inscrutable Look:
Magdalen

Life magazine, May 22, 1944, "Photo of the Week," by Ralph Crane: Her hair is perfectly styled, pinned up behind her with a huge flower. She wears a blazer, rests her chin on her left hand while her right hand holds a poised pen. In a perfectly proportioned composition, her head and right hand make two points of a triangle; the third, connected by the diagonal of her left arm, sits on the table in front of her: a human skull.

Subtitled "Arizona war worker writes her Navy boyfriend a thank-you note for the Jap skull he sent her," the photograph seems to offer yet one more instance of man's inhumanity to man from a war notable for its unparalleled destruction and brutality. The underlying rhetoric of racism that determined World War II

FIGURE 6: "Arizona war worker writes her Navy boyfriend a thank-you note for the Jap skull he sent her," *Life* magazine, May 22, 1944 RALPH CRANE/TIME & LIFE IMAGES/GETTY IMAGES

(on all sides) is well known, including the differing American attitudes toward the Japanese and the Germans. As one marine told John Hersey in 1943, "I wish we were fighting against Germans. They are humans like us. . . . But the Japs are animals." It is in this culture of pervasive racism and dehumanization that the problem of Japanese war trophies arises. As James Weingartner puts it, "If as a Marine Corps general noted, 'Killing a Japanese was like killing a rattlesnake,' then it might not seem inappropriate to detach something comparable to the reptile's skin or rattles for the pleasure of the victorious combatant and entertainment of his friends and relatives back home." The collection of Japanese war trophies—which included various body parts, including skulls—was, by all accounts, endemic and uncontrollable. Charles Lindbergh noted numerous such instances in the diaries of his travels to the Pacific theater: "It is the same everywhere I go," he wrote. The problem was so widespread that when Lindbergh returned to the States, he was asked by customs officers—almost as a matter of course—if he was carrying any "human bones" in his luggage. Crane's photo, appearing in one of the most popular magazines of the day, was only the most visible instance of a much deeper problem, one that was rooted in a long-standing program of propaganda that stretched back over a decade.

But Crane's photo stands out in its composition, which evokes the tableau of the memento mori, particularly Georges de La Tour's *Penitent Magdalen*. De La Tour painted this subject at least four times, each painting composed slightly differently, but always the silent, contemplative woman gazing at a human skull.

Mary Magdalen was a popular image in Renaissance art, and along with Jerome and Francis was most commonly depicted with a human skull. The common story at the time, that Magdalen had been a prostitute before meeting Christ, became a powerful narrative moment, as Magdalen is shown in de La Tour's paintings contemplating her mortal, earthly ways. As she holds the skull, she repents, turns her back on this life with its inevitable death in favor of an immortal life with Christ.

Crane's echo of de La Tour says a great deal about our relationship with death. In the Renaissance memento mori tradition, the skull is that sudden and uncanny disruption, an alien presence that infects its surroundings with the taint of mortality. By nature anonymous, it is an abstract figure of death, not any particular individual's remains. The tradition of memento mori is self-reflexive: One is meant to meditate not on the death of the skull's owner but on one's own death—the skull before the viewer is always and only the viewer's skull.

But the soldiers scalping their enemies' bodies were not thinking of their own deaths. In his novel *The Thin Red Line*, James Jones wrote of an "imagination problem," the problem being that American soldiers were unable to imagine their own deaths. One critic describes a scene in which the soldiers of Charlie Company are confronted with a report of the desecration of a fellow soldier's corpse, describing how "every soldier could imagine—but could not endure imagining—himself as that abject figure. And so each resorts to some mental strategy to magically forestall undergoing such a ritualized physical humiliation." Most avoid the fear of death by resorting to an ever-increasing brutality. "Obviously," one character remarks, "the only way really to survive in this world of humansocalledculture we had made and were so proud of, was to be more vicious, meaner and more cruel than those one met." It is precisely in acts of savage brutality that these American soldiers avoid facing their own mortality, as if, by becoming themselves inhuman, they can avoid the fate awaiting all humanity. The war trophy—the skull collected by Natalie Nickerson's boyfriend—no longer reminds the American sailor that he will die. It now assures him instead that it is the Japanese soldiers who have died and will continue to die.

The Renaissance tradition offered up one skull that was not anonymous, that had an identity, that most famous of skulls, Yorick's. Hamlet's soliloquy on the former court jester is an act of reclamation, rescuing Yorick's skull from a pile of anonymous bones and giving it a name and a history. In the process, Hamlet transforms it from an abstract memento mori into the trace of a specific person.

The most famous line in the soliloquy—"I knew him well!"—would find its way into a literary work that came out of World War II tackling the problem of war trophies. Winfield Townley Scott's poem "The U. S. Sailor with the Japanese Skull" details the process by which a head becomes a skull. Skinned, gutted, dragged behind a ship in a fishing net, and finally bleached white in the sun, the skull in Scott's account evolves until it is "made elemental, historic, parentless by our Sailor boy," a sailor who cannot now, after all that work, say, "Alas! I did not know him at all."

A poet and literary critic by trade, Scott fell into journalism during the war just to make ends meet, and in the process he saw much of the depravities of World War II firsthand. In the years following, he came to *Hamlet* as a way to comment on the barbarism of the Pacific conflict. Addressing a skull is always a confrontation with an uncanny otherness; in this case, the confrontation is with an other not divine but racial. Scott's poem uses the trophy skulls to reveal the always problematic relationship between human and dehumanized enemy. In the context of war, the iconographic figure of death itself is no longer as alienating as the more radical otherness of an enemy from another race.

Mostly Scott's poem is about *work*. Five of its stanzas call attention to the human material and labor that must be employed to create an anonymous symbol of death. The skinning and the scraping, the months in the fishing net as the salt water works the bone: The death's head takes time. Inverting *Hamlet*'s graveyard scene, Scott's sailor does not reclaim a nameless skull; he effaces an individual life, with all the violence present in such an act. Scott turns an abstract symbol that causes us to reflect on our own mortality and relationship with God into a meditation on brutality and savagery, one in which the savagery is projected onto the victim as an inhuman animal, explicitly as a means of avoiding that personal confrontation with death at the heart of the memento mori.

Published after the war, Scott's poem was a condemnation of the brutalities he had seen, but Crane's *Life* magazine photo, published during the heart of the war, had a different set of intentions. *Life* magazine was not quite outright government propaganda, but it definitely fulfilled an agenda in its presentation of the war. In particular, the magazine editors used captions and commentaries to guide their readers in how to read its photos. A May 1945 photo essay titled "The German People" used captions to create a specific narrative of the recently defeated Germans and their national character. The opening image of two teenagers and an older man is accompanied by a caption that reads, in part, "These faces are unhappy but hard and arrogant," in case the viewer finds their expressions inscrutable or enigmatic. This kind of ideological coaching, reducing the manifold possibilities of the photo to a single meaning, was an editorial hallmark of *Life* magazine.

But the encounter with the memento mori is always pedagogic. The entire concept of the memento mori is marshaled around its command function: Remember that you will die. In the seventeenth century, this function was made particularly clear in emblem books like George Wither's *A Collection of Emblems, Ancient and Modern*, published in 1635. Wither had come into possession of a book of emblems by the famous Netherland engravers, the van de Passe family but found their captions lacking. After writing a few new verses for some of the images, Wither was encouraged by friends to "moralize" the rest. Skulls appear prominently in nearly a fifth of the forty or so illustrations, and in almost every case, they are accompanied by variations on the same sentiment. "The rage of Death, which thou shalt see, Consider it, and pious be," reads one, while another reads, "Live, ever mindful of thy dying, For Time is always from thee flying."

One might expect this kind of pedagogic message in de La Tour's work as well. The iconographic significance of the penitent Magdalen was fairly well established by the time de La Tour produced his series of paintings on the theme during the 1640s. In addition to the skull, the paintings all feature the same set of symbols: the mirror indicating vanity, the burning flame symbolizing the soul in the process of purification, the chin resting on the hand to signify melancholic reflection, and so forth. To a seventeenth-century audience well versed in iconographic references such as these, the paintings would convey a familiar narrative, that of a former prostitute who contemplates her own mortality as she abandons the world of the flesh in favor of divine salvation, someone who'd taken messages like Wither's to heart. But the power of de La Tour's paintings may lie in the way they refuse the simple didacticism of an emblem caption: By focusing on the moment before the conversion, de La Tour refuses the look of gratified salvation, offering instead the enigmatic look of melancholy, which stands in mute tension with the pedagogic aim of the memento mori tradition.

What de La Tour's paintings and Wither's emblems suggest is that the memento mori tableau, however striking, cannot speak for itself and must be spoken for. Ralph Crane's photo for *Life* magazine appears to say something definite, something striking,

FIGURE 7: *Mary Magdalene with a Night Light* (1630–1635), Georges de La Tour LOUVRE, PARIS, FRANCE/GIRAUDON/ THE BRIDGEMAN ART LIBRARY

but exactly what it says depends on the caption underneath it. When the photo first ran in *Life*, it was accompanied by the following text:

> When he said goodby two years ago to Natalie Nickerson, 20, a war worker of Phoenix, Ariz., a big, handsome Navy lieutenant promised her a Jap. Last week Natalie received a human skull, autographed by her lieutenant and 13 friends, and inscribed: "This is a good Jap—a dead one picked up on the New Guinea beach." Natalie, surprised at the gift, named it Tojo. The armed forces disapprove strongly of this sort of thing.

It is difficult, in such a short paragraph, to get a clear idea of exactly how Natalie Nickerson felt upon receiving the skull or what was going through her mind as Crane took the photo; all we have of her mental state is the photo itself and the sentence "Natalie, surprised at the gift, named it Tojo." But, as with the caption of the "unhappy, hard, and arrogant" Germans, we're told how to read the image: The Japanese soldier is a "Jap" and thus unlike Nickerson's "big, handsome Navy lieutenant." Beyond this, the caption suggests a glibness, a cavalier attitude toward the skull, an editorial jocularity that is not reflected on Nickerson's face. If anything, she seems melancholic; she seems more like de La Tour's Magdalen than the magazine editors suspect.

The disjunct between the jocularity of the caption and the

detached quality of Nickerson's expression is striking. It's not clear, especially after the space of so many years, to what degree the photo was staged. The tableau seems unmistakably arranged to mimic the memento mori paintings, but it's difficult to surmise how much influence the photographer had on Nickerson's facial expression. If her look was a natural response to the human skull before her, it would seem to conflict, however subtly and momentarily, with the seeming callousness with which she reportedly named it Tojo. Her expression, perhaps, marks an authentic confrontation with death more than a celebration of one more enemy soldier dead. If Nickerson's look was staged, it suggests that Crane as a photographer was more interested in mimicking the memento mori images of artists like de La Tour than he was in setting up an image that would bear out *Life*'s ideological aims.

Crane's photo, perhaps surprisingly, provoked significant outrage, not just among *Life*'s readership but among the armed forces as well. For the remainder of the war, high-ranking officers, such as the army's judge advocate general, Major General Myron C. Cramer, made repeated, if futile, attempts to force commanders in the field to put a stop to the practice of collecting war trophies. Genuinely offended by the indecency of the *Life* photo and aware of the violation of the Geneva Convention regulations that it represented, these few voices of reason also knew full well what an opportunity the photo provided for Japanese propaganda. It was for the latter reason, and not for the desecration of an enemy corpse, that Natalie Nickerson's "big, handsome Navy lieutenant" was ultimately reprimanded.

More outraged, of course, were the Japanese. On August 10, Crane's image was sent to Tokyo from Berlin, and the national response was shock, anguish, and vitriol. Crane's photo was reprinted throughout Japan as a symbol of American barbarism, most notably in Japan's largest daily, *Asahi Shimbun*, which editorialized:

> This is truly the picture in question that has starkly revealed true American barbarism. . . . We, as Japanese, find it difficult to bear looking at it. A prayer spontaneously wells from our hearts—a prayer of blessing for the spirit of that Japanese war dead. The next instant we feel indignation pressing fiercely within our breast. Even on the face of the American girl can be discerned the beastly nature of the Americans. Let us all vow the destruction of American savagery from the face of the earth.

Despite the unsettling nature of the image, I'm not sure I see "the beastly nature of the Americans" inscribed on the face of Natalie Nickerson, any more than I see in her the glib chauvinism that the *Life* caption suggests. Having spent years looking at this photo, I'm still not sure what one could read in her expression other than a private and inscrutable confrontation with death, an experience that is not easily translatable into nationalist rhetoric of any kind.

In 1933, the German-Jewish philosopher Walter Benjamin predicted that the caption of a photograph would become increasingly important; without it, he wrote, "all photography construction must remain arrested in the approximate." In the case of Crane's staged portrait of Natalie Nickerson and her Japanese skull, Benjamin's assertion seems undeniable; it is the caption that works to shoehorn a photo's otherwise ambiguous content into a stable ideological message. Divorced from captions and bombastic propaganda, an image defies simple, didactic meaning—arrested in the approximate, the image of Natalie Nickerson offers instead a silent and unspeakable confrontation with the dead.

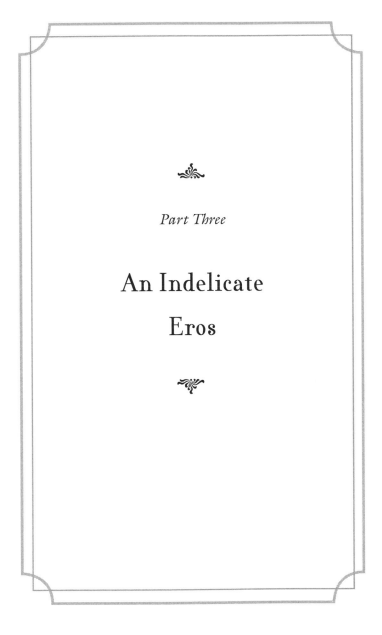

Part Three

An Indelicate
Eros

NINE

The Mother of
Pornography: Agatha

Medieval artists had very little use for breasts. In an age when the body was mainly the site of sinful pollution, and women in particular were considered inferior and not worthy of much attention, breasts were fairly maligned in much of early Christian art. When medieval painters did depict women, they portrayed them as boyish, their bodies nearly indistinguishable from those of their male counterparts. For the most part, women and men were distinguished on the basis of dress rather than physique. So for hundreds of years, breasts simply didn't enter into the iconography of the Christian church.

The lack of breasts complicates the depictions of one saint in particular, Agatha, who is noteworthy precisely for her breasts.

A noble-born woman traditionally said to have lived between 231 and 251, Agatha early on proclaimed her intention to remain chaste. One suitor in particular, a lower-class Roman prefect named Quintianus, grew frustrated by her resistance to him, denounced her as a Christian, and turned her over to the authorities. Hoping to break her of her chastity, Quintianus had her sent to a brothel, but even imprisoned there, she resisted the advances of the clients. At this point Quintianus had Agatha tortured, including the excision of her breasts, which, as it turns out, were miraculously restored with Saint Peter's help, so Quintianus finally had to have her executed. The story of the breasts became a central part of the story, though, which is why she's often depicted holding them on a tray or plate before her—if she once withheld her body from suitors and rapists, she now seems to offer it freely to us.

Like many saints, Agatha is defined iconically by her torture. But while her story was well known, it was rarely depicted in Western art. For being one of only seven female saints mentioned in the canon of the mass and patron of Sicily, her image is astoundingly rare. She wasn't portrayed with anything like the frequency of Catherine and her wheel, Sebastian and his arrows, or George fighting the dragon.

But then, it's hard to tell Agatha's story in pictures if you're not accustomed to depicting breasts. When breasts do appear, as in the case of the Virgin Mary or Jesus, they often signify nurturing, which clearly isn't applicable to the obvious sexual violence in the Agatha legend. And so, when she is depicted, she's often shown with her breasts already removed and with gaping wounds oozing blood on her chest.

So it's easy to understate the effect, in 1520, of Sebastiano del Piombo's depiction of Saint Agatha. Of course, by the Renaissance, breasts had reentered the picture, but Sebastiano's painting was among the few to represent Agatha's mutilation in such graphic terms. It remains unsettling, I think, not just because of its violence but because it so clearly borders on the pornographic.

FIGURE 8: *The Martyrdom of Saint Agatha* (1520), Sebastiano del Piombo PALAZZO PITTI, FLORENCE, ITALY/THE BRIDGEMAN ART LIBRARY

To invoke the word *pornography* opens up a whole hosts of issues that, once raised, will not go away. Not the least of which is what constitutes pornography itself—some five hundred years after Sebastiano's painting, most legal and cultural definitions still use some version of Judge Woolsey's famous comment: "I know it when I see it."

In its modern form, pornography emerges with the printing press. Erotic images and literature long predate Gutenberg, but only with the press did they become cheap enough to produce images and texts that could be, in a word, consumed. And so the primary distinction between the erotic and pornography, we could say, was one of class, age, and gender. Mature, upper-class men had long had what Walter Kendrick calls "secret museums" and considered themselves "responsible" enough to pore over their collections of erotica and read classical authors like Ovid. It was primarily the lower classes, children, and women who they feared could not keep control of themselves in the presence of such material. Put another way: The printing press allowed for the invention of pornography because it finally put a certain form of representation into the hands of those perceived to be too immature to handle it. So, historically speaking, a better definition of pornography might be: "I know it by seeing who sees it."

The fear about these vulnerable groups—the poor, children, and women—was that they were not sufficiently developed, morally, intellectually, or aesthetically, to keep control over their bodies. They are prisoners of their senses. To see pornography is to act, to be unable to keep from acting, and to act antisocially. Educated men, it was thought, could view pornography and restrain themselves, but these lesser social groups could not.

Curiously, in the early 1980s, Andrea Dworkin and Catharine MacKinnon inverted this traditional hierarchy, asserting that it was the men, not the women or children, who could not control themselves when confronted with pornography and who could not help immediately setting about raping women or committing other undesirable actions. For this particular form of second-wave feminism, the groups were reversed, but the relationship between pornography and prisoners of their senses and desires remained the same. It is the same debate that reappeared with regard to heavy metal in the 1980s and again after the massacre at Columbine High School with regard to violent movies and video games. The difference between us and them is that they have no control over their senses, and because of this they are dangerous and cannot be trusted with images that you and I can safely view and enjoy.

Of course, the story of Agatha and her tormentor Quintianus immediately presents itself as an allegory for this very problem. Agatha is aristocratic; she is pure; she deals with the abstract questions of the mind and the spirit. Quintianus is base; he is captivated by his senses; he sees the beautiful Agatha and cannot retrain himself. He must act. And he is, quite significantly, lower class—the class distinction in Agatha's story is not unimportant—the lower classes are dangerous precisely because they are uncontrollable and cannot control themselves. Agatha, resisting this lascivious, lower-class gaze, seems to me an allegory for a larger culture, perhaps the church itself, resisting or at least trying to resist the onset of pornography.

Pornography, after all, changed the ways other images were seen. Formerly innocent and innocuous art now took on a sexual charge, the most extreme example being a court case from the 1630s in which six Venetian patricians were formally charged with attempting to copulate with a statue of Jesus Christ. The ready dissemination of pornography had this effect; it took formerly saintly images and made them obscene. Linda Williams uses the term *pornotopia* to describe the mise-en-scène of porn narratives in which all characters and most objects are automatically sexualized—a situation Renaissance Italy found itself in with the sudden explosion of print technology. The saints, and even Jesus Christ, became the sexy schoolgirls, sexy nurses, and sexy nuns of their day. During the Council of Trent in 1563, it was noted that, with regard to any future sacred artwork, "all lasciviousness should be avoided, so that images shall not be painted and adorned with a seductive charm, or the celebration of saints and the visitations of relics be perverted."

Such a proclamation was forty years too late for Sebastiano, whose painting of Agatha was executed after the birth of print but before church authorities fully understood its underbelly. With Sebastiano's painting, the question is not just what are we looking at, but how are we looking at it? Do we see it as an exalted representation of the passion of the saints and through Agatha's martyrdom meditate on our own frail existence? Or is this just an early version of torture porn?

I wasn't sure what to make of this question for the longest time because I couldn't exactly say how I felt about Sebastiano's painting. I was moved by it, to be sure, but I was moved neither to piety nor to titillation. Finally I turned to an essay by Jill Burke, an art historian, offering a number of possible options for dealing with such a singular painting. Burke points out that most earlier representations of Agatha had shown her breasts already cut off; by showing the moment before the mutilation, Sebastiano is able to show her beauty as a whole. He also, against the protests of more prudish clergy, used statues of Venus as models for her, further equating her beauty with sexuality. So, exactly as they church might have feared, Sebastiano's painting seems to translate a moment of sublime suffering into something far more sexual.

To top it off, there is this knife in the foreground, recalling the verb *tagliare*, "to cut," a common euphemism for sex, specifically for the deflowering of virgins. But Burke notes that the knife is facing toward us in an almost threatening manner. So even as we are being titillated by Agatha's beauty, the knife may be reminding us of the dangers of giving in to such lust—its position suggesting that it can come for us as easily as for Agatha. This was a painting gifted to a cardinal, Ercole Rangone, who had taken a vow of chastity, though at the time, the sexual escapades of the clergy were legendary and the Vatican was being ridiculed for this hypocrisy. So perhaps this painting is a cautionary tale aimed at a particular clergy member, urging him to reject the lasciviousness of Agatha's torturers.

Failing that, at least Rangone could engage in a more "proper" lasciviousness, for the good cardinal was, in his time, legendary for his dalliances with his own sex. In one satiric poem of the time, the author writes that if he were elected judge in heaven, "I would have it that as many cocks as Rangone has had in his anus were held in front of him, and everyone could ask for his own mouthful!" Another verse in the same poem mentions a certain "Cavaglione's ass," "always a friend of service," that Rangone and others "frequently take in sodomy." Burke suggests that by painting such a blatantly erotic image for Rangone, Sebastiano may have been attempting to steer him away from the greater crime of sodomy; if he was going to screw around, at least he could find some ladies.

But no sooner has Burke offered this reading of Sebastiano's painting than she points out the strangely masculine character of Agatha—her broad shoulders, small breasts, etc.—suggesting that perhaps the inverse is true; Rangone is in fact incarnated here as Agatha. Burke ends this list of possible readings by suggesting that none of them is "true"; rather, an image such as this is always going to be ambiguous.

It is precisely this ambiguity that is bequeathed to us by this moment in which pornography emerged to flood and corrupt the visual lexicon. The once stable iconography of the church was opened up by a pornotopic gaze that sees sex in everything. And of course Agatha's torture, by its very nature, was particularly susceptible to this subversion. Breasts didn't really exist in Western art until precisely the moment when they became pornographic. The problem with representations of sexual violence is that even if we are asked to empathize with the victim, the painting can never fully guarantee that we will. You can make us look, but you can't tell us what to see. Here is the lesson of the saints, and of the images of the saints: that the lesson always gets away from us.

Pornography, particularly in the Italian Renaissance, was a stalking horse for a rising autonomy of the illiterate, the poor, the dispossessed—those who previously had been invisible. Sebastiano finished his painting at precisely the time when the church was losing its authority over its own imagery, when its monopoly of interpretation was breaking down. Interpretation, particularly of visual images, suddenly belonged equally to the uneducated and the marginalized. And while this was true of all representation, torture was and remains particularly vulnerable to "bad" interpretations by those with uncontrollable urges.

The passion of Agatha is perhaps really a struggle between high and low, between those in control and those excluded—the authorities and the pornographic viewer meet in this portrait of sexual violence, each struggling for the right to give voice to her silent screaming.

TEN

Unhidden Desires,
Unquiet Secrets: Sebastian

When it comes to the saints, the pornographic and the erotic are everywhere, and towering above them all, even more iconic than Agatha, is Sebastian. The image of Saint Sebastian comes naturally even to those who have never heard his name spoken. Painted countless times during the Renaissance, most notably by Guido Reni, he is impossibly beautiful: naked to the waist, hands bound above his head, his eyes placid but searching. But it is not his eyes that come to mind; it is his naked torso, pierced by a half-dozen arrows. The way Reni paints him, the arrows are fully in his body, no more than a few inches of the shafts protruding.

A Roman captain of the Praetorian Guard under Diocletian,

Sebastian had initially kept his Christian faith secret. But when two brothers named Mark and Marcellian were arrested for heresy, Sebastian could restrain himself no longer. After their parents tried to get the two brothers to renounce Christianity, Sebastian spoke up and not only strengthened their resolve but also converted their parents, Tranquillinus and Martia. Further, he converted the prefect Chromatius, who released the two brothers and his other captives. Sebastian went on to convert another prefect, Nicostratus, and his wife, Zoe. Zoe had been mute for six years, but upon her conversion by Sebastian she miraculously regained the power of speech. Unfortunately, due to his intercession, Mark and Marcellian were shortly killed, as were Chromatius; his only son, Tiburtius; and Nicostratus and Zoe. All were martyred.

Sebastian's persuasive talent leaves behind a trail of corpses: His golden tongue sows death and reaps martyrdom whenever he speaks. When Diocletian finally learns that a Christian is among his beloved Praetorian Guard, he sentences the young captain to death by firing squad. According to one account of his story, the archers "shot at him until he was as full of arrows as a hedgehog."

Among those struck by this story was Kimitake Hiraoka, who discovered a reproduction of one of Reni's paintings when he was twelve years old. By the time he wrote of his experience, he had taken the pen name Yukio Mishima, and his description of the experience in his autobiographical coming-out novel, *Confes-*

FIGURE 9: *Saint Sebastian* (1615), Guido Reni © CHELTENHAM
ART GALLERY & MUSEUMS, GLOUCESTERSHIRE, UK/THE BRIDGEMAN ART
LIBRARY

sions of a Mask, remains one of the great literary passages on masturbation:

The instant I looked upon the picture, my entire being trembled with some pagan joy. My blood soared up; my loins swelled as though in wrath. The monstrous part of me that was on the point of bursting awaited my use of it with unprecedented ardor, upbraiding me for my ignorance, panting indignantly. My hands, completely unconsciously, began a motion they had never been taught. I felt a secret, radiant something rise swift-footed to the attack from inside me. Suddenly it burst forth, bringing with it a blinding intoxication.

Despite publication of *Confessions of a Mask*, Mishima continued to maintain that he was straight. He eventually took a wife and fathered two children, keeping his homosexual identity somehow secret from his family and the public—though, as *Confessions of a Mask* suggests, he was dying to tell anyone who would listen. Whether Mishima was straight or not, his attraction to Sebastian marks that moment of collision between sexuality and death; the eroticism for Mishima is exactingly in the violence of the image: "The arrows," he writes, "have eaten into the tense, fragrant, youthful flesh and are about to consume his body from within with flames of supreme agony and ecstasy." It is a textbook moment of eroticism. According to Georges Bataille, a writer

Mishima very much admired, eroticism is the assenting of life up to the point of death, which reopens "the abyss that death once revealed."

But there is a problem. See Sebastian again, his body pierced by arrows, driven deep, puncturing liver, kidneys, lungs. Sebastian, despite these wounds, does not die. We think of this moment as his martyrdom, but Sebastian does not die by arrows. When the widow Irene comes to retrieve his body, she finds the maker of martyrs still alive.

Sebastian is secretly nursed back to health by Irene—whose own martyrdom is coming soon. Everyone who touches and is touched by Sebastian is marked for death, and Irene, too, will soon join the catalog of wreckage he leaves behind.

Convalescing, Sebastian continues his conversions. The power of his voice knows no bounds. But Sebastian can no longer stand being the one left alive while he sentences those around him to death. While he's staying at Irene's house, he gets word that the Emperor Diocletian is passing through the streets outside, and Sebastian goes to Irene's balcony and begins shouting at the emperor, calling him a murderer, a coward, a heretic. This is why he's been kept alive, why Irene rescues him: so he can heckle and insult the emperor. How must Sebastian have looked to his former boss, who had assumed him dead, and to his former comrades, who had shot him full of arrows? Miraculously resurrected, yet stupidly daring them to kill him once more. This is how he is captured by Roman soldiers a second time; when they storm

Irene's house, he does not resist. He's been waiting for this moment—he's already had practice at martyrdom. This time, they beat him with clubs—savagely. They beat him until he is dead.

I have no image of this to draw from. Unlike the arrows, the saint's being beaten to death was not a thing to be painted. If anything, I picture the scene in Scorsese's *Casino*, when Joe Pesci is taken to a cornfield and, along with his brother, stripped to his underwear and beaten by five men with aluminum baseball bats. The wet, flat slapping of the bats against Pesci's fat, the thud as he's thrown on his brother's body in the shallow grave, the dust coating the blood on his face, like flour on a greased pan, as they bury him alive. This is how Sebastian dies: It is not beautiful; it is not erotic. It is death, and it is brutal. They beat him, and then they throw his body in the sewers.

But if this is his real martyrdom, why do we only see him impaled by arrows? The confusion dates to the tenth century, when the first cycle of frescoes to depict the life of Sebastian was painted in the church of Santa Maria in Pallara. The frescoes depict five scenes from his life—the archers attempting to kill him, his convalescence at Irene's house, the disposal of his body in the sewer, the transportation of his corpse to the catacombs, and the burial. Notably missing in all this is his actual martyrdom, and over the ensuing centuries that omission was repeated until people assumed that it was the arrows that had done Sebastian in.

But there is another, more important reason for this misunderstanding: When Sebastian finally died, he was clothed, and it was his nudity that won him fame. Other than Christ, Sebastian was one of the few male nudes deemed an acceptable subject in the Renaissance and as such became a common image. Vasari relates that when Fra Bartolommeo was chided for not being able to paint nudes, "he did a nude St. Sebastian with very good flesh-coloring, of sweet aspect and great personal beauty, so that he won great praise among artists." Bartolommeo's Sebastian was so good, in fact, that while the painting was on exhibit in a convent chapel in San Marco, "the friars found out by the confessional that women had sinned in regarding it, owing to the realistic skill of Fra Bartolommeo."

Mishima could have told you that it wasn't just the nuns you had to worry about. Oscar Wilde may have been the first to refer to Sebastian as the "many penetrated saint," but throughout the twentieth century, he increasingly became a gay icon. In 1913, sexologist Magnus Hirschfeld listed paintings of Saint Sebastian in the first tier of images that especially appeal to the homosexual, and in 1976, Derek Jarman removed any lingering doubt with his first feature film, *Sebastianne*, in which the homoeroticism of the saint is made explicit and which—at this writing—marks the only time an erect penis has ever been shown on the BBC. Sebastian is the patron saint of secrets hiding in plain sight, secrets that are invariably about the ecstatic, erotic aspect of death, the beauty of a youth impaled by arrows.

But something else lingers after this unhidden secret, something that Yukio Mishima, for one, found out at the last. He had long dreamed of his own suicide, which finally came about on November 25, 1970 (not long after he'd staged a photograph of himself as Sebastian). After Mishima disemboweled himself, his former student and lover, Masakatsu Morita, stepped forward to decapitate him, completing the ritual of *seppuku* and the writer's beautiful, erotic death. Except that Morita, unskilled as a swordsman and overcome with emotion, was unable to swiftly and neatly behead his teacher—he hacked at the neck twice, succeeding only in making a grisly mess, before another of Mishima's students stepped forward to finally decapitate the writer.

So if all you see of Sebastian when you close your eyes is his perfect, serene beauty, remember always that after his eroticized death comes this other, far uglier thing, this second death, brutal, with little eros or redemption. It, too, is hiding, also in plain sight.

ELEVEN

A Multitude of Demons
and a Solitary Vice: Anthony

In many ways, the saga of Anthony and his temptations stems from a short scene from the Gospels that reappears in Mark, Matthew, and Luke: When the rich man comes to Jesus to ask what he must do to inherit eternal life, Jesus replies, "Sell all that you own and distribute the money to the poor, and you will have treasure in heaven; then come, follow me." Anthony was among those who heard the story of the rich man and took it seriously, though then as now it was a difficult passage to make sense of, particularly in cultures that see wealth and commerce as perfectly compatible with piety. Jesus's comment is not just about a disdain for money and worldly goods; it's about withdrawal, a removal from exchange and commerce, a solitude and isolation. Likewise, Anthony has continued to be a difficult saint to make sense of, one who's intrigued and confounded artists and writers in the centuries since, a saint of multitudes and of madness.

The main account of Anthony, a young nobleman from third-century Alexandria, comes from an early theologian named Athanasius who may have met him once but would later claim to have been a close disciple. Like any biographer, he aimed not at an objective record of facts but at a tightly constructed narrative with a pedagogical aim.

As Athanasius tells it, Anthony makes the decision to give all his worldly possessions to charity—which includes dropping his sister off at a convent—and wanders out into the desert. He takes up residence in a tomb carved into the side of a mountain, and there he is tempted by the devil. The devil begins by reminding him of his "guardianship of his sister" and the "bonds of kinship," hoping to smash Anthony's spiritual resolve with visions of the life he's abandoned. But these exhortations fall on deaf ears.

The devil then turns to lust, relying on "the weapons in the navel of his belly" to engage the hermit, but visions of luxurious women and at least one young Nubian boy also fail to stir Anthony. So the devil turns to fear and sends a horde of demons to physically attack the monk. Athanasius relates how, "approaching him one night with a multitude of demons," the enemy "whipped him with such force that he lay on the earth, speechless from the tortures. He contended that the pains were so severe as to lead one to say that the blows could not have been delivered by humans, since they caused such agony." In what was to become a hallmark of the Anthony story, Athanasius describes how these demons appear as a menagerie of terrifying animals: The demons "were changed into the forms of beasts and reptiles. The place immediately was filled with the appearances of lions, bears, leopards, bulls, and serpents, asps, scorpions and wolves, and each of these moved in accordance with its form." When Jesus was tempted by the devil in the desert, it was just the two of them, but hordes of intermediaries attack Anthony.

This conflict is not staged as an internal, psychological battle between faith and doubt: These events are external, visible to passersby. "Since he did not allow them to enter," Athanasius tells us,

> those of his acquaintance who came to him often spent days and nights outside. They heard what sounded like clamoring mobs inside making noises, emitting pitiful sounds, and crying out, "Get away from what is ours! What do you have to do with the desert? You cannot endure our treachery!" At first those who were outside thought certain men were doing battle with him, and that these had gained entry by ladders, but when they stooped to peek through a hole, they saw no one, and they realized then that the adversaries were demons. They were frightened and they called Anthony, and he heard them, but he disregarded the demons. And coming close to the door, he urged the men to be on their way and not to fear.

What to make of Anthony's torments from a contemporary perspective? Dubious of demonic possession, a modern etiology might assume him to be the sufferer of ergotism, a fungal poisoning char-acterized by hallucinations, or even epilepsy, which might account for his convulsing, raving body. Indeed, Anthony would eventually become the patron saint of both epilepsy and ergotism. He is the patron saint, one could say, of those whose bodies are given over to some other force—be it of godly, demonic, or biological origin.

The first half of the narrative is taken up by the demons who assail Anthony. But Athanasius wanted to make sure it was clear that our monk was beset by other temptations in the form of he-retical misinterpretations of Christ's message. "In things having to do with belief, he was truly wonderful and orthodox," we are told. "Perceiving their wickedness and apostasy from the outset, he never held communion with the Meletian schismatics. And neither toward the Manicheans nor toward any other heretics did he profess friendship, except to the extent of urging the change to right belief, for he held and taught that friendship and association with them led to injury and destruction of the soul."

Athanasius is quite clear on this—Jesus may have dined with prostitutes and moneylenders, but associating with heretics is surely a way to one's damnation. Pointedly, Anthony's final words in Athanasius's narrative are warnings about encroaching, alterna-tive interpretations of the Gospels:

> He called to those who were with him . . . and said to them, "I am going the way of the fathers, as it is written, for I see myself being summoned by the Lord. . . . You

know the treacherous demons—you know how savage they are, even though weakened in strength. Therefore, do not fear them, but rather draw inspiration from Christ always, and trust him. And let there be no fellowship between you and the schismatics, and certainly none with the heretical Arians. For you know how I too have shunned them because of their Christ-battling and heterodox teaching."

This is how Anthony supposedly leaves the world, railing against heretics whom Athanasius saw as dangerous. This is, after all, only the third century, and the Catholic Church has not yet crystallized into a single voice of authority. Dozens of differing factions are warring over the true meaning of Christ and his words, so it's not surprising that Athanasius employs Anthony to articulate the single, true path. This parallel structure, in which demons are replaced with heretics, is hardly coincidental; the two halves of the work reflect each other, painting a portrait of a righteous man beset on all sides by temptations. Anthony is thus the one who is inundated, and inundated by multitudes and multiplicity. His hallmark is the excess of temptations, a plurality without limit that threatens the single, solitary path.

Nor will demons and heretics be the only two categories of troubles to beset Anthony in the years to come. Again and again, we find him fighting off hordes and groups of different kinds as his story is recycled in different epochs. In fact, we might go so far as to suggest that Anthony's temptation is itself multiplicity: What threatens him is a deviation from cultural unity to multiculturalism, from the orthodox to the heterodox. Alone in the desert of your own mind, cut off from family and community—that's when you are the most vulnerable to wild deviations and divergences, to the manifold voices of temptation.

In the year 857, annals from Western Germany describe how "a Great Plague of swollen blisters consumed the people by a loathsome rot, so that their limbs were loosened and fell off before death." This is the first recorded instance of ergotism, an alkaloid poisoning caused by fungal infections in rye. In addition to the gangrenous symptoms, ergotism can cause vomiting and diarrhea as well as central nervous disorders, leading to spasms and convulsions. It can also cause hallucinations: In the early 1930s, the primary alkaloid ergotamine was synthesized and given the name lysergic acid, which Albert Hofmann would shortly use as the basis of LSD. Prior to the identification of this fungus, however, ergotism was commonly interpreted as demonic possession or bewitchment—recent scholars have gone so far as to argue that the Salem witch trials may have been spurred by an outbreak of ergot poisoning.

In 1095, the son of the French nobleman Gaston of Valloire was afflicted with this horrible condition until he was miraculously cured by the remains of Anthony at the Benedictine priory of

Saint-Antoine l'Abbaye. Whether or not these were actually the remains of the saint is to be debated; the nearby Saint-Julien in Arles also claimed to have a complete set of the saint's relics, as if the hermit's body itself was miraculously multiplying. But the bones at Saint-Antoine were good enough for Gaston, who was so impressed by his son's recovery that he founded the Hospital Order of Saint Anthony, a congregation of monks that was devoted to curing ergotism, plague, and other skin diseases. It was in this manner that ergotism came to be known as "Saint Anthony's fire." It is also how Anthony became associated with epilepsy, whose symptoms often mirrored ergotism and which was also taken to be the result of demonic possession. Since pig fat was often spread on these wounds to soothe the irritation, Anthony was often depicted with pigs in the background, and his new role as the healer of skin diseases was assured.

As the Antonine Order spread and its influence grew, the popularity of Anthony the Great grew throughout Europe. The next major representation of Anthony's temptation came with the publication of *The Golden Legend*, a collection of narratives about the saints, in the mid–thirteenth century. Here again, the multitude of demons was stressed, though the *Legend*'s take differs slightly; Now the beasts are described not by name but by their anatomical characteristics: "And anon they came in form of divers beasts wild and savage, of whom that one howled, another siffled, and another cried, and another brayed and assailed St. Anthony, that one with the horns, the others with their teeth, and the others with their paws and ongles, and disturned, and all to-rent his body that he supposed well to die."

This shift seems slight on a descriptive level, but it was enough to usher in a dramatic change in the representations of Anthony and his troubles. In the following years he became a popular pictorial subject, and as painters in the fifteenth and sixteenth centuries turned to Anthony more and more as a subject, new figures begin to appear. In the late fifteenth century, Martin Schongauer depicted him as lifted into the air by these demons, and while the horns, teeth, paws, and ongles are all there, we are far from the identifiable list of animals that Athanasius listed.

Schongauer's image was copied by a twelve-year-old Italian named Michelangelo in what would be his first painting, but it was in northern Europe countries that images of Anthony and his temptation reached their fullest expression. The most well known of these is the triptych by Hieronymous Bosch, painted in about 1505. Whereas earlier Roman and Byzantine images of Anthony had placed him squarely as the focus of the image, staring head-on, benevolent and full of wisdom, Bosch's Anthony is lost in the sea of fantastic creatures and demons that afflict him. In the left panel he is held aloft by the bat-like creatures tormenting him. He appears again in the foreground, his body broken and attended to by followers who nearly obscure him altogether. He has regained his composure in the center and right panels, though his half-turned posture in both makes exegesis difficult. In the right panel, he turns away from Lust as she emerges from a tree, but does his turning result from his steadfast resolve, or is he more tempted by the bizarre and sinful figures before him on the table? In the center panel, he gestures toward the tiny crucifix in the middle of the painting, but is his look meant to exhort us to follow his example, or is he giving in to the demons all about him?

Roughly five years later, Matthias Grünewald would revisit this scene with his altarpiece for Isenheim. Grünewald's masterpiece is well known for his horrifying image of Jesus Christ afflicted with sores—an image that has become a sort of shorthand in art history surveys for, to quote one textbook, "symbolic expression" through vivid "gesture and color." But if Grünewald's Christ is horribly wracked by skin disease, it is because Isenheim was a monastery for Antonine monks, and Christ is here suffering from Saint Anthony's fire. Indeed, it is the desert ascetic, not Christ, who is the true heart of the altarpiece. He appears to the right, his staff bearing the symbol of his order, flanking Christ along with Sebastian, patron of plagues. When the altar's first set of wings are opened, more peaceful scenes of Christ's annunciation are depicted, but there is yet another set of wings, and when the altarpiece is fully opened, the innermost images are of Anthony—on the left meeting with Paul the Hermit and on the right undergoing his temptation. As in Bosch's triptych, Anthony is nearly overwhelmed by the demons attacking him, but his expression is far from that of the placid, contemplative saint who easily resists these torments in Bosch's work. As the German writer W. G. Sebald described the scene,

To him, the painter, this is creation,

image of our insane presence

on the surface of the earth,

the regeneration proceeding

in downward orbits

whose parasitical shapes

intertwine, and, growing into

and out of one another, surge

as a demonic swarm

into the hermit's quietude.

In this fashion Grünewald,

silently wielding his paintbrush

rendered the scream, the wailing, the gurgling

and the shrieking of a pathological spectacle

to which he and his art, as he must have known,

themselves belong.

Why did Anthony's torments become such a fruitful ground for painting during this time? Why are we so drawn to monsters and grotesques? The importance and significance of this subject and its emergence in the Renaissance are best explained by Michel Foucault, who uses the temptation paintings as points of departure in his history of madness. They appear, he argues, precisely at the point at which madness is introduced into the Western world, and they are emblematic of this shift. Previously the world of nature was clearly and inextricably linked with a stable system of symbols: The nightingale stood for melancholy, the ermine for purity, and so on. At least since the Book of Genesis, when Adam names the animals brought to him by God, the natural world had been seen as a clear and readable text by God—all creatures large and small belonged to a hierarchy of symbolic meaning, and this symbolic structure had remained stable for centuries.

But with the sixteenth century, the idea of madness first appears and begins to break all this apart. No longer does reflecting on the natural world allow for wisdom and transcendence; now that natural world is an impenetrable cipher. This comes about not from a loss of meaning but from an overload of meaning. "Things themselves," Foucault writes, "become so burdened with attributes, signs, allusions that they finally lose their own form. Meaning is no longer read in an immediate perception, the figure no longer speaks for itself; between the knowledge that animates it and the form into which it is transposed, a gap widens."

The image of Christ, for example, is no longer the simple, unalterable picture of triumph over suffering since it is now burdened and overburdened with so many kinds of suffering. Now he is not just crucified—he suffers from ergotism, or is it plague, or epilepsy? That pig by Anthony's side—does it indicate the pig fat used to cure skin diseases, or has Anthony become the patron saint of swineherds? How has our ascetic hermit, who wanted only to be left alone, become the patron saint of basket-makers and brush-makers, of gravediggers and lost items, of butchers and domestic animals? He is assailed by yet another multitude, this time one of patronages. But he is not alone; in such a plethora of attachments, iconography veers toward the meaningless, as does the whole world of symbols that once were self-evident, each giving way to a cacophony of possibilities.

It is for this reason that the temptation paintings, with their wild, uncontrolled bestiaries, come to have such importance. It is the very nature of Anthony's story that tells the story of madness. Unlike those saints who are iconically associated with one distinct object—Sebastian with his arrows, Lawrence and his gridiron—Anthony is associated with plethora itself, with a multitude that can take any shape. Thus, it is his story that becomes paramount, and the beasts that surround him, with their increasing strangeness, give expression to a world in flux—our world.

In the early Renaissance, Foucault continues, "the beasts were let loose, and they made their escape from the world of legend or moral instruction and took on a fantastical life of their own." The Renaissance was an age of hybrid monsters: butterflies with the heads of cats, owls with lobster claws, monstrous figures that defy any explanation. The creatures that torment Anthony are only the most visible expression of this breakdown—made up of recognizable elements, bits of animals whose individual meanings might be known, these hybrid creatures nonetheless stubbornly resist interpretation as the forms collide into a cacophony.

If the beasts that torment Anthony seem haphazard, partial, out of alignment, it is because they no longer represent stable symbolic forms but instead offer only the fragments of an unknowable nature. More so than ever, we understand only that we don't understand, that the world exceeds our grasp. For Foucault, this is where madness takes hold in the Western imagination, between the incomprehensible image and the multiple, contradictory meanings retreating behind it. Perhaps madness can bridge this gap—the madman just might understand the meaning of these creatures, but that is an esoteric, terrible knowledge that cannot be put into words.

"Madness also exerts a fascination because it is knowledge," Foucault writes. "These strange forms belong from the outset to the great secret, and Saint Anthony is tempted by them because he has fallen prey not to the violence of desire but rather to the far more insidious vice of curiosity." In these paintings, we see Anthony still beset by a multitude, but not of heretical sects; the multitude here consists of fragments of once symbolic forms, unmoored from that symbolism and set loose to wander. Or, looked at another way, the multitude consists of all those endless and hermetic forms of knowledge that lie beyond the grasp of the human mind. And if the temptation is now that much more tempting, if the Anthony depicted by Bosch and by Grünewald seems closer to giving in than Athanasius ever imagined, it is because the visual world itself has given into temptation—it can no longer maintain a single, orthodox meaning.

In the beginning was the Word, the Gospel of John tells us, and the Word was with God. And for a time, the Word held dominion over the visual. But art is itself now excess and madness; it is the multitudes of the visual sign freed from the Logos. Anthony is tempted by this, too—the multiplication of the visual image that inundates the univocal Word of God. This estrangement between word and image is permanent; we will never heal this rift, and the visual image with its excess of meaning will henceforth threaten that writer who seeks the single and just word that names the world. Images confront the writer as the demons confront Anthony, tempting him into madness.

B y the seventeenth and eighteenth centuries, our approach to madness had undergone a shift. The mad were locked up in asylums along with the unemployed, prostitutes, blasphemers, and other misfits—those, in other words, who had failed to become productive members of society. As market capitalism developed in the Western world, the most dangerous element was those people who could not be assimilated into its new economies—the madman was not so much ill as he was useless. Worse, his uselessness was potentially contagious, and so it had to be contained.

More and more, a suspicious eye was turned toward those pursuits that encourage this uselessness, idles and pleasures that led impressionable women and children away from their societal duties and into time-wasting and fantasy. But what most needed to be prevented was precisely the kind of solitary introspection of someone like Anthony. The stories of Jesus and the rich man and of men like Anthony who could take it seriously and walk away from commerce were no longer welcome in the burgeoning capitalist landscape. In the new economy, withdrawal was punished; in the new economy, everybody pays, and everybody plays.

Of course, one of the chief vices in this regard is the novel, particularly the realist novel. There is nothing physical about a novel—it consists of no raw material, no labor, no surplus that can be touched or resold, no exchange. All the work that is done, all that is produced, is in the mind of the reader—a closed loop that takes you out of the world of production and into the dangerous desert of solitary imaginings. In the words of an anonymous article from 1768, "The existence of so many authors has produced a host of readers, and continued reading generates every nervous complaint; perhaps of all the causes that have harmed women's health, the principle one has been the infinite multiplication of novels in the last hundred years. . . . A girl who at ten reads instead of running will, at twenty, be a woman with the vapors and not a good nurse." Impressionable readers could not be trusted to tell truth from fiction, reality from novel.

If there is a posterwoman for this problem, it is Gustave Flaubert's Emma Bovary. As a young girl in a convent, Emma devours saints' biographies and romances, missing the moral instruction and fixating on the sensual images: "She had loved the church for the sake of the flowers, music for the words of the ballads, and literature for its power to kindle her passions; but her mind rebelled against the mysteries of faith, as she became ever more irritated by the discipline, which was a thing alien to her temperament."

This inability to get the lesson, to take to her conditioning, to put her time to good use, in turn creates a dangerous imbalance in her, leading to her dissatisfaction with her husband's bourgeois provincialism, to her adultery, to her suicide, and all the rest—all of Madame Bovary's problems can be traced to a fixation on fantastical narratives and images that have no place in reality. Indeed, when it comes to her first extramarital infatuation, the young law student Léon, she prefers dreaming of him to his actual presence: "She was in love with Léon, and she sought solitude, the better to take her pleasure undistracted, in images of him. The actual sight of him upset these voluptuous meditations. Emma trembled at the sound of his footsteps; and, in his presence, the emotion subsided, leaving her with only an immense astonishment that finished in sadness." Emma's crime is only secondarily adultery; her real transgression is her surrender to the madness of novels, to the endless production of virtual images that have no correlation with the reality around her.

The danger of the reader is that she (for it is always a she) conjures fantasies and images that have no real correspondence with reality; she engages in romance, in fantasies—she creates a surplus, a fictitious capital of images. None of these have exchange value, none have use value, and so they corrupt and defile.

It was the creation of this woman obsessed with fantastical images that won Flaubert both fame and infamy—not just her story but the finely detailed, exacting prose that set the stage for the modern realist novel. This is the writer who, famously, nearly drove himself mad searching for *le mot juste*, the perfect word, the single expression that could tame and corral the visual imagination of his reader. As recently as 2008, critics like James Wood were still making the case for Flaubert's influence: "Novelists should thank Flaubert the way poets thank spring," he writes; "it all begins again with him. There really is time before Flaubert and a time after him. Flaubert decisively established what most readers and writers think of as modern realist narration, and his influence is almost too familiar to be visible."

Thank not just Flaubert but his friends Louis Bouilhet and Max Du Camp, who steered him away from dangerously abstract romanticism toward the minutely detailed life of Emma Bovary. In the fall of 1849, the then unknown Flaubert invited Bouilhet and Du Camp—his two closest friends—to join him for a reading of what he believed would be his masterpiece, a retelling of the temptation of Anthony. The thirty-year-old writer had been working on *The Temptation* for four years, and he was excited finally to share it with the two men whose opinion he trusted most. Bouilhet and Du Camp were likewise excited. Even though Flaubert had yet to publish anything, they both knew of his extraordinary talent and were anxious to hear this masterwork, to be present at the first airing of a project that had consumed their dear friend for so long.

Flaubert told them beforehand that he wanted their honest

appraisal of the work. But just before he began, the author waved the manuscript pages in the air above his head and exclaimed, "If you don't howl with pleasure at this, you're incapable of being moved by anything!" Settling down, he began to read.

He read the entire manuscript straight through, all 541 pages. Eight hours a day, in uninterrupted four-hour blocks of time, for four solid days. During that entire time, as he read his opus, these men whom he most loved and trusted—Maxime Du Camp and Louis Bouilhet—sat in silence.

They would later remember those four days as the most painful in their lives. What they heard was no masterpiece but an unending morass of words that was by turns incomprehensible, banal, repetitive, childish, and plain boring. "As he read," Du Camp recalled,

> Flaubert warmed, but we, though we tried to share his enthusiasm, remained cold as ice. Words, words—harmonious phrases expertly put together, full of noble images and startling metaphors, but often redundant, and containing whole passages which could have been transposed and combined without changing the effect of the book as a whole. There was no progression—the scene always remained the same, though played by different characters. We said nothing, but Flaubert could easily perceive we were not favorably impressed, and from time to time he interrupted himself to cry: "Wait! Wait! You'll see!"

After it was over, they did their best to put a good face on the experience, to let Flaubert down easily. But that was a difficult task, as they clearly felt that the author's last four years (and their own last four days) had been wasted on something unsalvageable. With as much tact as he could muster, Louis Bouilhet told Flaubert simply, "We think you should throw it into the fire and never speak of it again." Finally Du Camp, struggling to put a good spin on things, explained to Flaubert, "You proceed by expansion. One subject sweeps you toward another, and you end up forgetting the point of departure. A droplet becomes a torrent, the torrent a river, the river a lake, the lake an ocean, the ocean a tidal wave. You drown, you drown your characters, you drown the event, you drown the reader, and your work is drowned."

At their urging, Foucault agreed to abandon the abstract and focus on careful, detailed observations of real life, writing *Madame Bovary* in a fraction of the time he'd spent on his desert saint. But if the adulterous woman was what he was to become known for, it was the ascetic hermit that remained his obsession; even after his humiliation at the hands of his friends, he continued to be tempted by the romanticism of his Anthony story. After the failure of that first attempt, he went to Egypt on an extended voyage with Du Camp, who had won a commission from the Academie d'Inscriptions to photograph architectural antiquities there.

Accompanying Du Camp on such a mission was somewhat difficult for Flaubert since he disdained photography. Flaubert came of age in an era where culture was becoming increasingly visual—cheap lithographs and reproductions were available everywhere, and the new invention of photography was already vastly changing the cultural and artistic landscape. Flaubert hated all of it. For most of his life, he managed to completely avoid the camera's eye; he once wrote to his mother, "I would never allow anyone to photograph me. Max did it once, but I was in Nubian costume, standing, and seen from a considerable distance, in a garden." Indeed, Du Camp's photograph of Flaubert in the garden of the Hotel du Nil is the only known image of Flaubert as a young man. Flaubert's iconophobia was legendary; at the time, magazine caricaturists needed written permission from their subjects before publishing an image—a right that Flaubert never granted. As he told one illustrator, "I reserve my face for myself." And that he did. It seems almost inconceivable now that we have no definitive idea of what he looked like during most of his life, that someone of such historical importance managed so successfully to elude portraiture until well into his late life.

As realism became the dominant mode of fiction, novelists from Dickens to James had contentious relationships with visual culture. But Flaubert is a special case. He plays Anthony to the temptation of the visual world before him—he seeks the singular word of the god-like author, *le mot juste*, perfectly placed and immovable for all time. But this word is always under threat from photographers and hack illustrators. The estrangement of word and image that Foucault saw beginning in the Renaissance reaches its climax here, with Flaubert, the hermit-like author resisting the temptations of a thousand images.

An Indelicate Eros

But if Flaubert is a special case in this regard, it is because his loathing of the visual image went beyond his aesthetic. Put simply, Flaubert was terrified of images because he had epilepsy, and he believed that he had developed epilepsy because he masturbated, and he masturbated because he could not write his masterpiece, *The Temptation of Saint Anthony*.

Flaubert worked on the *Temptation* off and on from 1845 until the eventual publication of the third and final version twenty-nine years later, in 1874. It was never easy, and its production was an almost constant struggle. Often, out of frustration, he turned to masturbation, which he was fairly casual about describing. "I'm gnawed by anger, impatience, impotence," he confided to a friend. "There are moments when my head bursts with the bloody pains I'm taking over this. Out of sheer frustration I jerked off yesterday, feeling the same bleakness that drove me to masturbate at school, when I sat in detention. The ejaculate soiled my pants, which made me laugh, and I washed it off. Ah! I'm quite sure Monsieur Scribe never stooped so low!" Masturbation was a foil to good writing both literally and figuratively; in his letters to female friends, he likened the frustrations of writing to "masturbating his head" in order to "ejaculate" a few sentences at a time. And in 1855 he wrote, "We take notes, we embark on voyages . . . we become scholars, archeologists, historians, doctors, cobblers and people of taste. But what about heart and verve and sap? We're good at licking cunt. But humping? Ejaculating in order to make a child?" Above all, Flaubert wanted to *make* something, to be a productive member of literary society through a great and popular work. Nothing threatened this more than his own *Saint Anthony*. Flaubert's obsession with the hermit was too esoteric, too idiosyncratic. The nineteenth century wanted the realism of Balzac; it had no taste for the romance Flaubert sought to create. His was a perverse, solitary obsession, self-centered in its scope and taste—no wonder it drove him to self-pollution.

Flaubert was playing a dangerous game; in the nineteenth century, it was believed that masturbation presented far more serious dangers than simply bad writing. It was, quite simply, thought to be lethal. In the 1875 edition, Larousse's *Grand Dictionnaire* noted that "we find in the annals of medicine plenty of cases of five-, six-, and eight-year-old children dead as a result of masturbation." As Samuel Tissot, one of the foremost fighters against onanism, noted, "Too great a quantity of semen being lost in the natural course produces dire effects; but they are still more dreadful when the same quantity has been dissipated in an unnatural manner. The accidents that happen to such as waste themselves in a natural way are very terrible, those which are occasioned by masturbation are still more so." Masturbation, it was said, could lead to consumption or any number of nervous disorders, including epilepsy, which plagued Flaubert throughout his life. He suffered his first attack when he was twenty-one, on January 1, 1844, while riding in a carriage with his brother. With the onset of the seizure, Flaubert lost consciousness for ten minutes in what he later described as "torrents of flame" sweeping him away. He was to suffer from these episodes regularly throughout his life, and they so horrified him that he would never once use the word *epilepsy* to describe his condition.

By Flaubert's time, such an attack no longer bespoke divine or demonic possession; Flaubert's seizures were quite a long way from Anthony's body wracked and tossed about the tomb in a cataclysmic spiritual battle. Convulsions and spasms like Flaubert's were, rather, understood to be the result of a serious moral failing, an ethical rather than divine transgression. And Flaubert seemed to agree with Tissot's diagnosis—he confided to a friend once how "madness and lust are two realms I've explored so deliberately. . . . But I've paid a price for it. My nervous malady is the scum of these little intellectual pranks. Each attack has been a kind of hemorrhage of innervation."

Why did masturbation lie at the root of so much suffering? As Thomas Laqueur explains in his exhaustive history of masturbation, *Solitary Sex*, three things made onanism unnatural. First, it concerned a fantasy rather than a real object, and as such, "masturbation threatened to overwhelm the most protean and potentially creative of the mind's faculties—the imagination—and drive it over a cliff." Second, it was profoundly antisocial, or at least it was social "in all the wrong ways," as Laqueur suggests: "Wicked servants taught it to children; wicked older boys taught it to innocent younger ones; girls and boys in schools taught it to each other away from adult supervision." Third, it was uncontrollable; it could "neither be sated nor moderated. Done alone, driven only by the mind's own creations, it was a primal, irremediable, and seductively, even addictively, easy transgression. Every man, woman, and child suddenly seemed to have access to the boundless excesses of gratification that had once been the privilege of the Roman emperors."

We know now what Anthony was doing in that cave and why he was tormented for it. Alone, in the deserted privacy of the desert, phantasms multiply and corrupt the mind, and the seminal work of the recluse gives birth not to healthy children but to unnatural demons. Alone, the imagination goes into overdrive—it produces multitudes—the heterodox excess that tempts Anthony is also the insatiable imagination of the masturbator, an excess without limit or reserve.

But there was a deeper problem, particularly in those early days of the Industrial Revolution, for masturbation not only mocked traditional sexuality and marriage, it more insidiously parodied and threatened the developing system of market capitalism. Like credit, sexual fantasies could seem real but were in fact based on nothing. Behind every economic bubble lies the same masturbatory economy.

And behind them all also lies Emma Bovary and her production of useless images that satisfy nothing but their own excess, leading to self-destruction and madness. And Laqueur notes that novels in particular "were even more threatening than the world of commerce; they were more purely the counterpoint of masturbation. Markets, however wild and speculative, had a bottom line, however hidden; bubbles burst, credit collapsed. No reassuring reality principle governed the world of novels." On this point, our good Dr. Tissot was no fool; he knew full well that novels and their writers led down the dangerous road to self-abuse: "The self-polluter perpetually abandoned to his obscene meditations is in this regard, something in the case of the man of letters, who fixes all his attention on one point."

So it would seem that Emma Bovary, after all, is not so much an adulteress as a masturbator. And indeed, a hundred years after the novel's publication, another novelist, James Agee, put his finger on the button in a review of Billy Wilder's film *Double Indemnity*: "I have always thought—not very originally, I imagine— that the essence of *Madame Bovary* and her millions of great-granddaughters is masturbation, literal as often as figurative."

Reading and masturbation. Emma engages in both, literally and figuratively. In fact, the two vices are the same action: succumbing to a surplus of images that are not grounded in reality. Both threaten capitalism, and both were the lifelong pursuits of the epileptic Flaubert. Flaubert, who was to have begun a career in law and would have become a successful, productive member of bourgeois society. That is, before his epilepsy set in and spared him that fate.

Epilepsy, after all, is not just one of many illnesses that could result from the solitary vice; it is in many ways the most emblematic. The epileptic suffers from the nightmare form of the masturbator's plethora of fantasies: attacked by an endless, ergotistic series of hallucinations from which he cannot escape. Here's how

Flaubert explained it: "At twenty-one I nearly died of a nervous illness brought on by a series of irritations and troubles, by late nights and anger. It lasted ten years. (I have felt, I have *seen* everything in Saint Teresa, in Hoffman and Edgar Poe; people visited by hallucinations are not strangers to me.)" Flaubert was not Emma Bovary, in love with these useless images; he was Anthony, plagued by them, tormented by them.

In the 1848 draft of Flaubert's *Temptation*, Anthony speaks for his creator, describing his temptations in the language of the epileptic: "I felt desperately unable to control my thought; it slipped the bonds with which I had tied it and escaped me. . . . Like a rogue elephant, my mind would race beneath me with wild trumpetings. Sometimes I'd lean back in fright, or else boldly try to stop it. But its speed stunned me, and I'd get up broken, lost."

As Frederick Brown put it in his recent biography of Flaubert, "Since his memory for images was astonishingly retentive, mortal danger lay in those thrust upon him from without or in hallucinations independent of his will. The author who devoted himself stubbornly to a delirious anchorite was also the epileptic terrified of losing his mind and the lover fearful of being tyrannized by desire (all three combined to make up the man who, fighting shy of cameras, sat only once or twice, grudgingly and late in life, for a photographic portrait)."

Flaubert's terror of images and his refusal to have his work illustrated, his masturbation, his epilepsy—all tap into a moment of iconophobia in the nineteenth century, one that is still with us today. A fear of a surplus of images, of too many pictures, many of them free-floating and without referents, unable to be entered meaningfully into a system of commodities, of exchange and use value—this is the terrifying truth: that our modern society is based on nothing but fantasy. The capitalist, the reader, the masturbator cower in Anthony's cave, beset on all sides by endlessly replicating pictures of madness.

FIGURE 10: *Temptation of Saint Anthony,* from the Isenheim altarpiece (c. 1512–1516), Matthias Grünewald

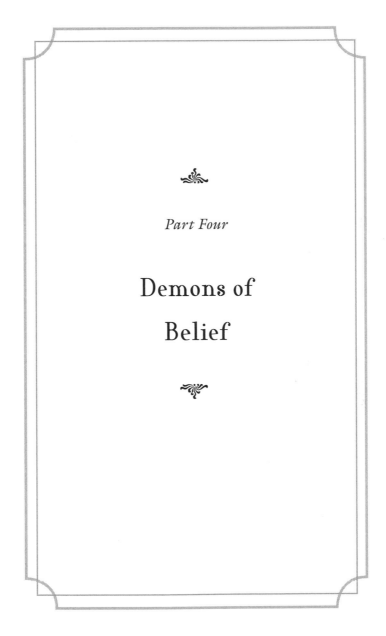

Part Four

Demons of
Belief

TWELVE

Legends of Sudden
Explosions: Barbara

It is easy enough to say one believes, or doesn't believe, in the saints. It is harder to say how one believes, or how one comes to no longer believe, in a saint. Depending on who's doing the counting, there are upward of ten thousand named saints; must one believe in them all to believe in one? The lives of some saints are so unreported that there is hardly more than a name, while others touched thousands, were photographed, walked among us. What does one do with the more distant saints, the ones who seem to spring from nothing more than legend passed down?

Among the many accounts of Saint Barbara's martyrdom is this one, written near the end of the twentieth century:

According to legend, our patron saint was the beautiful daughter of Dioscorus, a nobleman of the Roman Empire, believed to have lived in Nicomedia in Asia Minor in the third or fourth century, A.D. Because of her singular beauty and fearful that she be demanded in marriage and taken away from him, and also to limit Barbara's exposure to Christianity and encourage her development as a zealous pagan, her father kept her shut up in a tower. But even such incarceration could not keep the young woman from becoming a Christian.

When her father finally discovered Barbara's hidden faith, he flew into a rage, and then "the evil Dioscorus tortured his daughter Barbara, then took her to a high mountain, where he beheaded her. Afterward, as he descended the mountain, he was caught in a sudden violent storm, struck down and consumed by lightning. Only his scorched sword remained as a reminder of God's vengeance."

This account comes not from any Catholic source but from the United States Artillery Association and can be found in the manual *How to Conduct a Saint Barbara's Celebration*. The Saint Barbara's celebration "is recognized as an occasion where ceremony, tradition and good fellowship play an important part in the life of the Army officer. It provides an occasion for officers to meet socially, enjoy a ritual military meal, hear speakers of distinction, discuss subjects of military or national importance and honor those in their midst who have achieved notable accomplishments." The only limits to a Saint Barbara celebration, we're advised, "are the imaginations of the planners and good taste," though planners "should never forget that each of these activities ought to retain the dignity essential to achieving the common objectives of all Saint Barbara's Day celebrations."

Why does the United States Artillery Association, of all organizations, take Saint Barbara as its patron? After Dioscorus's sudden immolation, the manual explains, "Barbara came to be regarded as the sainted patroness of those in danger from thunderstorms, fire, explosions—that is to say, sudden death. Given the questionable reliability of early cannon misfires, muzzle bursts and exploding weapons were not uncommon—it is easy to see why our predecessors sought the protection of Saint Barbara. She has protected us well ever since."

Nor is the USAA alone in this tradition; in French and Spanish naval terminology, the archaic word *saint-barbe* was used to designate the powder magazine on battleships. The British poet G. K. Chesterton commemorated the Battle of the Marne in his 1922 poem, "The Ballad of Saint Barbara," with verses like this:

The touch and the tornado; all our guns give tongue
together,
St. Barbara for the gunnery and God defend the right,

and

She is risen for all the humble, she has heard the
   conquered calling,
St. Barbara of the Gunners, with her hand upon the gun.

For Chesterton, it is "Barbara of the batteries" who can be relied
upon in times of war, whose explosive force keeps the free world
free. She is not the only military saint, but she is the saint of the
cannon, of the powder, of the sudden and convulsive explosion.
Saint Barbara, who blows things up for justice.

The odd cultural history of Barbara reveals that, often, what is
far more important than the saint is the story of the saint.
Jacobus de Voragine's thirteenth-century collection of hagiographies, *The Golden Legend*, brought the saints into the public's
imagination like nothing before it. It became the standard reference work for saints throughout the Middle Ages and the Renaissance; when the martyrs and confessors were depicted in
Renaissance art, or when Elizabethan writers like Shakespeare and
Milton referenced them in allusion and metaphor, it was Jacobus
they followed.

Despite *The Golden Legend*'s popularity at the time, reading
it now can be a dreary experience. The stories start to bleed together: Jacobus frequently omits or ignores all particularities of a
saint's life so that after a while, they seem generic. We assume this
is deliberate, an attempt to make each saint universal. As part of a

series of mostly indistinguishable lives, then, each saint became most associated with whatever single attribute might differentiate him or her from the rest—Catherine's wheel, Lawrence's gridiron, and so on.

Barbara had been venerated as a saint and martyr for centuries before Jacobus, but it was *The Golden Legend* that made her real, put her story on paper definitively and gave her a body. Even so, the details of Barbara's life are sparse, and what little Jacobus gives us is mostly forgettable: She was a great beauty, her father was a pagan, and she was martyred for her faith. Unlike Catherine or Lawrence, she suffered no grand, idiosyncratic torture, beheading being a fairly common mode of death in *The Golden Legend.*

What was to become most iconically associated with her happened *after* her death, when her father, Dioscorus, was killed by lightning on his way back down the mountain. Sudden death, freak explosions—these are what start to cling to Barbara.

And then, two hundred years after publication of *The Golden Legend,* a house caught fire and burned to the ground. Its owner, Henry Kock, was horribly burned in the fire and, by all accounts, shouldn't have been able to make it out. According to the *Catholic Encyclopedia,* Kock "was nearly burned to death in a fire at Gorkum. He called upon Saint Barbara who aided him to escape from the burning house and kept him alive until he could receive the last sacraments." Because of Kock's story, Barbara became someone you could call on to prevent sudden death, who would intercede to keep you alive until you received last rites. She became one of the Fourteen Holy Helpers, the key medieval saints who were most efficacious in day-to-day affairs (including Denis, invoked against headaches; Elmo, for abdominal problems; Christopher, for plague; and so on).

I wanted to know more about Henry Kock, so I went looking for additional information. I wanted some snippet of biography, some small specificity that could make him come alive. He appears repeatedly in descriptions of the miracles of Saint Barbara, particularly to explain how her name became associated with deliverance from sudden death, but it's always the same line, over and over—"A man named Henry Kock was nearly burnt to death in fire at Gorkum; he called on St. Barbara, to whom he had always shown great devotion. She aided him escape from the burning house and kept him alive until he could receive the last sacraments." Occasionally this brief passage appears with slight variations, but nowhere did I find more than this.

Perhaps Henry Kock exists only in reference to Saint Barbara, like a phantasm that haunts her story. Perhaps not. I can't say with confidence that Henry Kock was a real person who was burned horribly in a fire; nor can I say that he wasn't. If he was real, all that remains of him, like the burned frame of a house after a fire, is this one statement.

Three hundred years after Henry Kock's reported death, on the evening of June 20, 1745, the Veronese countess Cornelia Zangari de Bandi of Cesena burned to death. As recorded by the prebend of Verona, Reverend Joseph Bianchini, the countess was sixty-two years old on the night of her death. The evening was not unusual: She retired at a normal time, spent some time talking to her maid, then said her prayers and went to sleep. When the maid went to wake her the next morning, she found the countess's "corpse on the floor in the most dreadful condition. At the distance of four feet from the bed there was a heap of ashes. Her legs with the stockings on remained untouched and the head half-burned lay between them. Nearly all the rest of the body was reduced to ashes." The scene was noteworthy in that many details defied conventional understandings of pyrotechnics: "A small oil lamp on the floor was covered with ashes, but had no oil in it, and, in two candlesticks which stood upright upon a table, the cotton wick of both the candles was left, and the tallow of both had disappeared." The bed was disturbed as if she had just risen, but neither it nor any other item in the room showed any trace of fire.

Stories of spontaneous human combustion date back at least as far as 1613, to a carpenter named John Hitchell of Hampshire, England. Still lying beside him in bed, his wife awoke one morning to find him smoldering. An inextinguishable "smoke of mist" rose from his body for three whole days until his body was consumed. In 1725, in Rheims, a man named Millet was initially accused of murdering his wife but was acquitted through expert testimony from some local physicians who argued that the wife had died from spontaneous combustion.

But in the nineteenth century, this particular mode of death truly caught the imagination of the public and came to be seen as an especially terrible way to die. The Countess de Bandi's case was reported widely and was held up most often as proof that spontaneous human combustion was a real and prevalent threat. Charles Brockden Brown's 1798 gothic novel, *Wieland*, features a death by spontaneous combustion, and the essayist Thomas De Quincey confessed a terror that his addictions might lead to "anomalous symptoms," including spontaneous combustion. "Might I not myself take leave of the literary world in that fashion?" he wondered. Then the specter of spontaneous combustion captured an even brighter literary star.

Charles Dickens had already established himself as a master of realism and social commentary when he began serializing his masterpiece *Bleak House* in 1852. A scathing indictment of the Chancery legal system in England, the ill-treatment of the poor, and the degradation of Britain's class-based society, the novel is notable for the thirtieth chapter, in which a minor character—the alcoholic landlord Mr. Krook—spontaneously bursts into flames.

For a writer so thoroughly committed to realism, the introduction of such a bizarre manner of death struck many as an unforgivable blemish on the novel. Dickens's friend and fellow writer George Lewes was aghast at the scene and used his weekly column in *The Leader* to savage Dickens: "The death of Krook by Spontaneous Combustion is certainly not an agreeable incident, but it has a graver fault than that of 'shocking' people with 'sensitive nerves;' it is a fault of Art, and a fault in Literature, overstepping the limits of Fiction, and giving currency to a vulgar error." Lewes was careful to distinguish the supernatural (the ghosts in *A Christmas Carol*) from the improbable: "In the one case, Imagination and our mysterious sympathy with the Unknown are appealed to, without pretence of claiming more than imaginative credence; in the other case, the Understanding is called upon to ratify as a truth what it rejects as falsehood." Lewes's problem was that spontaneous combustion appears in the novel not as a fantastical device but as realistic: "Even supposing Clairvoyance and Spontaneous Combustion to be scientific truths, and not the errors of imperfect science, still the simple fact that they belong to the extremely questionable opinions held by a very small minority, is enough to render their introduction into Fiction a mistake. They are questions to be argued, not to be treated as ascertained truths."

Dickens shot back immediately, appending a preface to the next installment of *Bleak House* claiming that among "men of science and philosophy," there was much "learned talk about inflammable gasses and phosphuretted hydrogen." Dickens cited the case of the Countess de Bandi as well as a few others, hoping that would end the matter. It did not.

"What you write is read wherever the English language is read," began Lewes's response in his next column. "This magnificent popularity in turn carries with it a serious responsibility. A vulgar error countenanced by you becomes, thereby, formidable."

Lewes then responded to Dickens's proof with a battery of medical experts who dismissed Dickens's sources as "humorous, but not convincing!" Dickens had relied on his own expert—Dr. John Elliotson, educated at Cambridge and former professor at University College, London—who had provided him with a number of facts and evidence for spontaneous human combustion. But Elliotson also believed in the similarly disputed science of phrenology, and he had left the University College Hospital in order to found something called the Mesmeric Infirmary. Despite this, Dickens sent another private letter to Lewes heavily quoting Elliotson, detailing more spurious evidence and cases of more women who'd caught fire and died.

Lewes gave up shortly thereafter, unconvinced but exhausted, but Dickens did not relent. When *Bleak House* appeared as a novel in September 1853, he included a preface that argued once more for the truth of the spontaneous combustion phenomenon, adding, "I have no need to observe that I do not willfully or negligently mislead my readers and that before I wrote that description I took pains to investigate the subject." He claimed that there were at least thirty cases on record, though he named only the Bandi story and the same few others Lewes had already dismissed. Dickens ended by observing, "I shall not abandon the facts until there shall have been a considerable spontaneous combustion of the testimony on which human occurrences are usually received."

As with any spurious medical condition, belief in spontaneous human combustion persisted because it tapped into deeper, psychological fears: fears of being alone, getting older, becoming useless to society. When Pierre Lair, in the *Journal du Physique*, made a catalog of common attributes of victims of spontaneous human combustion, certain trends emerged: Victims were usually women; they were usually over the age of sixty and often overweight. Most important, nearly all of them were alcoholics. In Dickens's letter to Lewes, he repeatedly pointed to alcoholism as a cause of combustion when it came to "women in the decline of life." "Refer to the Annual Register for 1773 for the case of Mary Clues—a woman of fifty, and a drunkard," he wrote. "To the Transactions of the Royal Society of London for the case of Grace Pitt—a woman of sixty; not stated to be a drunkard, but not likely to have been a lady of very temperate habits, as she got out of bed every night to smoke a pipe, and had drunk an immense quantity of spirits within a few hours of her death. Refer to Le Cat for the case of Madame Millet who got drunk every day"—indeed, it was evidence of Madame Millet's alcoholism that helped get her husband acquitted of murder.

Though the scientific evidence clearly held spontaneous human combustion to be impossible, the connection with alcoholism seemed to make intuitive sense, and people clung to it. As the temperance movement gained steam, spontaneous combustion found new life as a dangerous consequence of imbibing too much alcohol; in February 1863, the *Pennsylvania Temperance Recorder* reported that the blood from an alcoholic could be set on fire, and similar reports continued to circulate well into the twentieth century. The importance of excessive drinking became the central component in reports of spontaneous combustion. Just as masturbation could cause a physical, violent death among children who practiced it wantonly, so, too, could alcoholism cause a violent, fiery death in an era in which social and ethical lapses often had immediate, physical consequences.

As late as 1928, Dr. W. A. Brend's well-respected *Handbook of Medical Jurisprudence and Toxicology* contained this entry for spontaneous combustion:

> Spontaneous combustion of the body, in the sense that the layman attaches to the words, never occurs; but, very rarely, a state of the tissues exists for which Dixon Mann suggests the term preternatural combustibility. The condition has been most frequently noticed in the bodies of fat, bloated individuals who have been excessive drinkers. Probably, in such cases, inflammable gases are generated in the body after death, and, if a light is near, become ignited, leading to a partial consumption of the soft tissues.

Only with the repeal of Prohibition in America and the death of the temperance movement worldwide did spontaneous human combustion finally fade from medical discussions. Writing in the *British Medical Journal* in 1938, Dr. Gavin Thurston noted, "One can picture the temperance fanatics making much of the phenomenon of spontaneous combustion and pointing out the foretaste in this world of the fate which awaits the drunkard in the next." But like John Hitchell's long-smoldering body, belief in spontaneous combustion lingered on. In 1945, the *Transactions of the Medical Society of London* confessed that "we are entirely in the dark as to the real nature of the chemical changes which give rise to this state, but it seems reasonable to infer that they are in some way or other connected with the long use of alcohol."

And then, on January 6, 1980, another strange event in the annals of spontaneous human combustion occurred. Constable John E. Heymer of Ebbw Vale, South Wales, was summoned to the apartment of one Henry Thomas, whose remains had recently been discovered. "As I gazed at the surprisingly small pile of ashes and the disembodied feet," Heymer later wrote, "I was reminded of the scene of Krook's death by Spontaneous Human Combustion in Dickens' classic *Bleak House*. I was certain that I was looking at such a scene."

Heymer has spent much of the last thirty years arguing that spontaneous human combustion is a real phenomenon, on television and in magazines devoted to conspiracy theories and wherever else anyone will listen. Despite his fervor, he does not refer to himself as an outright believer; rather, he calls himself an "askeptic."

Dickens, after all, revealed the dangers of being a true believer in spontaneous human combustion. With all of *Bleak House*'s penetrating social commentary, memorable characterizations, and skillful plotting, Krook's death remains to modern critics (as it was to Lewes) an embarrassing misstep, a blight on what might otherwise be a perfect novel. Whether or not Dickens ever changed his mind about spontaneous human combustion, contemporary readers are left with this rather awkward detail. Literature ages differently than nonfiction, and even if no one believes in spontaneous human combustion any longer, we are stuck with Dickens's belief in it.

And Saint Barbara? Should we believe in her? Jacobus certainly did when he included her in *The Golden Legend*. But like the word *legend* itself, the meaning of her story has evolved through the centuries. The word *legend* (from Latin, meaning "something to be read") first came into the English language through translations of *The Golden Legend* and in its original usage meant simply the life of a saint. When Geoffrey Chaucer published his collection of Greek and Roman lives, *The Legende of Good Women*, he broadened its meaning to any kind of story or history. But it was not until the seventeenth century, according to the *Oxford English Dictionary*, that it came to mean "an unauthentic or non-historical story, especially one handed down by tradition from early times and popularly regarded as historical." Barbara's life, too, once assumed to be purely factual, is now generally seen as largely mythical.

How does a saint's life become an unauthentic or nonhistorical story? Partly it has to do with the invention of the printing press, which sparked a newfound fascination with the objective truth of the written word. With the explosion of print, documents could be spread far wider and could be compared and evaluated beyond one's local community.

In time, Barbara's life, and her very existence, fell victim to this spread of information. Multiple stories of Barbara's martyrdom gave the place of her death as Nicomedia, Heliopolis, Rome, or Antioch—when these stories were exchanged, the inconsistencies cast doubt on the truth of the underlying story. Ultimately, the lack of any concrete, verifiable detail doomed the saint. The 1907 edition of *The Catholic Encyclopedia* was still willing to entertain the notion of Barbara as a real individual, though a year later, *The New Schaff-Herzog Encyclopedia of Religious Knowledge* began its entry for Saint Barbara with the line "A saint whose career belongs to the domain of legend."

This skepticism toward Barbara put her sainthood at increasing risk through the latter half of the twentieth century. Among the reforms that came out of the Second Vatican Council in 1962 was the reform of the liturgical calendar, in which was agreed that, henceforth, "the accounts of martyrdom or the lives of the saints are to accord with the facts of history." Pulling the saints from myth into fact, the bishops of Vatican II set about putting an end to the saints of legend in favor of men and women whose existence could be verified. The process took years, but the liturgical calendar saw the disappearance of a number of prominent saints, among them Saint Christopher and Saint Barbara. The bishops, unable to find any historical proof for the existence of these saints, deemed them products of unsubstantiated legend.

Those who revered the newly decanonized saints were naturally outraged, and the church immediately backpedaled, stressing that while the acts of the saints like Barbara could not be verified, the subsequent veneration of these saints was still very real. Thus, while removing them from the official liturgical calendar, the church left the veneration of these saints to local calendars.

Sometimes what remains is not the saint but the belief in the saint. Sometimes what remains is not the fact but the belief in the fact.

Sometimes, ashes.

THIRTEEN

Violent Jokes and
Stolen Bones: Foy

Future readers, I warn you not to be thrown into confusion by the way this work is organized and not to look for a chrono- logical sequence of events." So begins Bernard of Angers's chron- icle of the miracles of Saint Foy. After all, how *could* one begin with Saint Foy? Not with her life, of which not much is known— only that she was a French virgin from Agen who was no more than a girl when she was martyred in the late third century. So few details of her life exist that many historians suggest she may in fact may have been fictitious. Her name, Foy, after all, simply means "faith"; while the name was not uncommon, Foy's story may have been meant as a metaphor for faith generally rather than as the life of a specific young girl.

Nor can we begin with her death, since her story tends to repeat the same generic details one finds in so many virgin martyrs' deaths. Even if she was a real person, there's little to Foy's story that distinguishes her, and so, like Bernard of Angers, we must begin much later, not with her life or her death but over seven hundred years later, 120 miles from her home. There Foy found fame in the regions surrounding the monastery of Conques, where the strange list of miracles attributed to her relics begins.

As a miraculous healer, Foy seemed most concerned with sight—in return for devotion, she regrew the once-gouged eyeballs of a man named Guibert: "At about midnight," Bernard tells us, "it seemed to Guibert that he saw two light-filled globes like berries, scarcely larger than the fruit of a laurel tree, which were sent from above and driven deeply into the sockets of his excised eyes." No word from Bernard on how an eyeless man saw those globes in the first place; nonetheless, when Guibert awoke the next morning, his eyes had returned. When a bandit similarly had his eyes gouged out after a robbery gone wrong, he wandered, suicidal, through the forest until a young girl appeared to him and drew two eyes from her cloak, which she thrust into his ruined sockets.

Many miracles attributed to Foy are even more fantastic, including her fairly idiosyncratic talent for resurrecting animals. Her chroniclers list at least four occasions when Foy miraculously brought to life dead mules and horses. She also, true to form, repaired the eye of a knight's horse after it had been gouged out on a spike. Explaining these equine miracles, Bernard comments that "we maintain our hope of human resurrection with greater certainty if we see that animals, which are inferior to men, are sometimes raised from death."

Foy's miracles were so common throughout the region of Conques, and so bizarre, that the nobility began referring to them as Foy's "jokes": There was the time, we're told, that she cured a woman of an "offensive blemish of warts"; there was her miracle baldness cure, when a knight prayed feverishly and was rewarded with a head of hair "so rosy red in color that people thought the whole top of his head was stained with fresh blood"; and there was the time that Foy miraculously conjured a hammer in order to free a peasant who'd been long imprisoned.

An even greater hammer-related miracle took place in Auvergne when one bold warrior became inflicted with a hernia: "During periods between the old moon and the new," another chronicler explains, "a portion of his intestine left its proper place and ruptured into his scrotum with a great roaring of his bowels." Praying fervently to Saint Foy, the warrior was finally rewarded with a vision in which she said to him, "You should know that although I have cured serious ailments caused by many different diseases, I've never been called upon at all to treat the kind of problem you bring to me." But Foy, ever generous, offered this advice to the ailing warrior: He was to go to the nearest blacksmith, lay his scrotum out across the anvil, and have the blacksmith strike it with a hammer that has been heated until "it is glowing white." Half believing the saint was mocking him, the miserable knight nevertheless dragged his wounded scrotum to the blacksmith and instructed him to pound on it with a white-hot hammer. The blacksmith would have none of it, telling him, "Believe me, my lord, these weren't the words of a healer but of some joker. If you are naïve enough to follow this advice, you could be accused of your own murder. And I will never enact such an evil crime, for I am completely convinced that you will meet an instant death with this."

The knight, though, would not be dissuaded. He promised the blacksmith that he would hold him blameless. As the chronicle then relates: "What more is there to say? His swollen scrotum was stretched out over the anvil and his diseased genitals were prepared for the blow. Soon the blacksmith flexed his muscular arms and swung the enormously heavy hammer high into the air. When the warrior saw what awaited him he was struck with incredible terror, slipped backward, and lay prostrate, as if all his bones had been broken in a fall to his death. And in this headlong fall, wondrous to report! All at once his herniated intestines were sucked back inside so completely that they never ruptured again for the rest of his life."

So this is how one approaches Saint Foy, through odd stories in which she helps criminals, bald men, and horses while playing practical jokes on herniated knights. There's a lawlessness about Foy's work, a petty and churlish quality, as humorous as it is bizarre.

But there's also a dark undercurrent in her jokes, one that frequently veers into the vindictive. Take, for example, the man whose roof collapsed on him shortly after he declared the monks of Conques to be "a pile of shit." Or the young nobleman Pons, who Bernard of Anger describes as having a "pallid face, rolling eyes, gnashing teeth, and flailing fists," and who set out to ambush Foy's monks after a taxation disagreement. On his way to attack, "a spherical cloud veiled the serene sky and, after a sudden horrifying and menacing rumble and a huge flash of fire, an arrow from heaven pierced the man's brain." Recounting this story as one more proof of Foy's miracles, Bernard triumphantly crows, "Your corpse can't even serve as food for wild animals and birds." Or, lastly, take the monk who blasphemously declared that Saint Foy had no need of wine before attempting to steal from the monks' cellars. "At that very moment," we're told, "his muscles lost their ability to move and stiffened completely; the wretch lay paralyzed on the ground, his arms and legs drawn up to his body. In addition, his mouth was stretched back to his ears and gaped obscenely, and the filth that streamed foully from his entrails manifestly revealed how harshly and distressingly he had been afflicted." With a flurry of redundancy, Bernard concludes, "So the wretch, tortured with wretched torture, scarcely extended his wretched life, wretchedly, for more than two days."

Foy, for all her saintliness and miracles, is vengeful and violently protective of the monks who guard her relics. Perhaps this has something to do with how she arrived at Conques. The relics of a martyred saint, after all, were the most valuable possessions of the Conques monastery, and their importance cannot be underestimated. It was the relics of the saints and martyrs that, quite literally, put the whole ancient and medieval world in motion. These skulls, fingers, and other body parts created donations, made or broke cities, sent people traveling, launched wars. They comprised one of the main central economic engines of the premodern Christian world.

For a long time, Conques did not have its own saint, which put it in a precarious economic position. The monastery was intended originally as a stop for pilgrims on the road to Santiago de Compostela, but in the ninth century, Pepin I of Aquitaine realized it was a bit too remote to serve that purpose adequately. He founded another monastery at Figeac, which was soon being called "the New Conques." Facing their impending obsolescence, the monks at the original Conques decided that they needed some important relics to increase their visibility and draw pilgrims back to their monastery.

In 855, they sent a monk named Audaldus to Valencia to acquire—by whatever means necessary—the remains of Saint Vincent of Saragossa. Having dug up the saint's relics, Audaldus was on his way out when he was caught with the relics by the bishop, who tortured Audaldus, confiscated what was left of Saint Vincent, and sent the monk back to France. Returning home, he found that his fellow monks refused to believe him; having been savagely tortured on their behalf, he was in turn expelled from Conques by his less than forgiving brethren. Now homeless, Audaldus wandered until he arrived at another monastery, in Castres—which, it turns out, had more resources at its disposal. There Audaldus convinced his new brothers simply to buy the remains of Vincent of Saragossa outright, which is how they ended up in Castres rather than Conques.

Conques, meanwhile, was still without its saint. Unable to get Vincent of Saragossa, they decided next to try to acquire Saint Vincent of Pompéjac—one Vincent being apparently as good as the next. For this, they sent another monk to Agen, where the second Vincent's remains were kept. More successful, Conques's new relic hunter passed himself off to the monks at Agen as a secular priest and was admitted into their order; according to one report, he spent ten years gaining the trust of the Agen monks before being appointed guardian of their relics. Only then could he break into the tomb of Saint Vincent of Pompéjac and steal his remains. He apparently decided, while he was at it, also to take the remains of Saint Foy.

Around the same time, the monks at Figeac—Conques's rival monastery—liberated some relics in an attempt to further one-up Conques. A Figeac monk later wrote that his order was "always eager to acquire the bodies of saints by trickery or theft" and finally succeeded by taking advantage of the siege of a nearby city to carry off the remains of its patron saint, Saint Bibanus.

Such actions were not considered thefts at all. The term for this process was *translation*, and, indeed, such translations were almost universally praised and considered acts of Christian virtue. The nameless Figeac monk's comment suggests that there was little attempt to cover up the illegality of these acts—for many, the theft of a saint's relics and their translation to a final resting place was seen as a necessary component of that saint's official story. The fact remained that most believed it was through God's intercession that such a theft could occur in the first place; thus, by implication, God sanctified these translations. It was the very fact that these monks were able to break the eighth commandment and get away with it that proved the holiness of their mission.

No one proved this more fully than Foy herself. Her story begins in holy criminality, and so, too, were many of her miracles defined by a sacred lawlessness, her ability to reach down from heaven to wreak violence in order to protect her relics and the monastery that housed them. When a local bishop's nephew, a man named Hugh, was kidnapped, the bishop decided to steal Foy's bones and trade them for his nephew. He had stolen her remains and was on the way to Hugh's captors when Foy appeared to the bishop in a vision and proclaimed, "I come from Gourdon Castle, where I myself have just killed Hugh, the one whose ransom was to be paid today with my treasures."

It's hard to reconcile tales like these with the story of a pure, virgin martyr. The story of the child who sacrificed herself rather than deny her faith, after all, is far more attractive, and it is the story that the people of Conques would prefer you to remember. It was this child saint whom the writer Hannah Green fell in love with when she came to Conques in the late 1970s, spending a good deal of the rest of her life working on a book about Foy.

"Sainte Foy could be quite fierce," Green wrote in *Little Saint,* "and her fury could be final; she could be a warrior when she had to be, but for the most part she took on the character of a charming child, affectionate and loving and lovely, young lady, girl of almost thirteen, full of gaiety and humor, going after, for instance,

FIGURE 11: Reliquary statue of Saint Foy (c. 980) CHURCH OF SAINT FOY, CONQUES, FRANCE/THE BRIDGEMAN ART LIBRARY

the jewels of special beauty that she wanted, as if it were to satisfy her feminine vanity. So she lived out in her miracles in the people's minds the rest of the young years she had denied herself."

Maybe, but I'm not so sure. I also see the dark, dangerous side to Foy, the saint who embodies the kind of lawless vigilantism that is always popular in times of political and social upheaval. I see a patron to the nihilistic visions that seize us in times of uncertainty, and she offers no answers save her own power; she's chaotic, petty, and deadly, and the only consolation she can offer us is in the belief that she's on our side. In his justification of her violence and her jokes, Bernard of Angers advises us, "We shouldn't judge divine work with human reason; we should firmly believe that it was done." He tells us to trade reason for faith—for Foy—and submit ourselves to her jokes, or rather to submit ourselves to the holy men who claim her violence as their own; to submit ourselves to stories written after the fact, in which murder and violence are recorded as divine intercession. Of all the saints, the only one I truly fear is this young girl from southwestern France, the virgin martyr who restores your eyes even as she demands your blindness.

FOURTEEN.

The Monstrous
Saint: George

Much of the actual life of George, like those of Barbara and Foy, is lost to history, if he was in fact a real person. He was, from the beginning, a fantastical saint, not one you could put much faith in—a common euphemism for such saints is that their deeds are "known only to God." Even as early as the fifth century, skeptics had begun to cast doubt on his existence, including Pope Gelasius (492–496), who complained that George's life appeared to have been written by a heretic designed as a "pretext for casual mockery" of the early church.

Gelasius had a point. Early accounts of George's life were fanciful, straining all limits of credulity—particularly the story found in a document known as the *Vienna Palimpsest*, where the earliest account of George's martyrdom can be found. A Roman captain like Sebastian, George was well liked by the Emperor Datanius but was forced, like all other Christians, to sacrifice to pagan gods to prove his loyalty to the emperor and to renounce his faith. When George was unable to do this, the emperor had him tortured in all manner of ways. According to the *Palimpsest*, George was forced to wear iron boots into which nails had been hammered, his head was beaten with a hammer, a red-hot helmet was placed on his head, more nails were pounded into his head, his skin was pierced with iron hooks, he had molten lead poured into his mouth, he was placed inside a bronze bull lined with nails and spun around, and then he was set on fire.

This was just the beginning. George was killed three separate times and resurrected three times by the Archangel Michael so he could undergo more torture. During this orgy of violence, George managed to raise some 460 people from the dead and convert them, miraculously producing water from the ground for their baptism. He turned the throne of the emperor into a fruit-bearing tree, cured a child of blindness, and resurrected an ox. The molten lead poured into his mouth did not stop him from summoning and directly engaging Apollo, whom he forced to confess that he was not a real god. When George was finally beheaded, a rain of fire consumed his tormentors, an earthquake terrified all who remained, and then milk and honey flowed from his corpse.

It's easy to see why Gelasius and others were so quick to discount George. The absurdity of these tortures makes a mockery of martyrdom, substituting for a life-and-death moment a cavalcade of goofy violence so extreme yet disembodied that it feels like a Looney Tunes cartoon.

Of all the tortures recorded in the *Vienna Palimpsest*, though, the most fascinating is the one involving the bronze bull. Assuming, as Pope Gelasius certainly did, that most of the tortures listed in the *Palimpsest* are invented, this one in particular is a curiously literary touch since anyone who heard it would immediately have thought of an earlier pagan story that was well known throughout the Roman Empire. That story involves the king of Crete, Minos, who, along with his wife, Pasiphaë, was cursed by the gods (according to different sources, either he offended Poseidon with his hubris or she offended Venus by failing to make offerings). As punishment, Pasiphaë developed an unnatural lust for one of Minos's bulls, and had the king's mechanical genius, Daedalus, build a wooden cow covered in hide that she could fit inside. In this manner Pasiphaë had sex with a bull and ultimately bore a son—the half-human, half-bull Minotaur.

Pasiphaë, to Minos's great shame, is the mother of a monster born of an unnatural desire. The *Vienna Palimpsest* recasts George the martyr as an echo of Pasiphaë, as though he, too, is on the verge of giving birth to something monstrous, something beyond the understanding of the human mind.

The cult of George is a study in the evolution of a belief across continents and across cultures. He was originally popular throughout the Middle East and had shrines and churches dedicated to him in Cairo, Antioch, Syria, Constantinople, and Lydda in Palestine (his supposed birthplace). His name means "worker of the land"; from his earliest days, he was a saint of agriculture, and he was largely unknown in Europe.

All this changed with the Crusades. In 1098, European Christians attempted to sack the city of Antioch, which had a shrine to George at its gates. According to the crusaders' story, as they descended on the city, a vision appeared of three knights on white horses, carrying white banners—the saints George, Demetrius, and Mercurius, who led them to victory over the city's Muslims.

George soon became a favorite saint of the crusaders, who claimed he helped them to spread Christendom in his native land by force. Accordingly they brought him back to Europe on their return and began to build shrines and churches for him through-out their homelands. But it was Jacobus de Voragine and *The Golden Legend* that truly cemented his reputation: George's story is one of the longest in the entire book, and it is the first appear-ance of the story of George and the dragon. In this version, George was a wandering knight who happened upon a town somewhere in the desert of Libya that was besieged by a dragon. The townspeople had been regularly offering sheep and human sacrifices to appease it when, by lottery, the king's own daughter was chosen. George heard her cries and attacked the dragon, driv-ing his lance into its side and commanding the young girl to throw her girdle around its neck. As the girdle landed on the dragon, the creature became instantly docile, and George and the princess were able to lead it back to town on a leash.

George, it should be said, was far from the only saint to deal with dragons. Saint Margaret of Antioch was swallowed by a dragon, so the story goes, but when she held up her cross in the belly of the beast, he disgorged her. Saints Matthew, Donatus, and Martha all also faced and defeated dragons. The dragon is a regular feature in these stories because it was a recognizable symbol of evil for many European audiences, and these encounters with dragons would have been largely read as symbolic. But what made George's story particularly popular was the fact that he was a knight. Jacobus was writing during the burgeoning age of chivalry, when the concept of the heroic knight was appearing in popular romances, particularly in France and England. Jacobus's version of George appropriated those secular stories, subordinating the chivalric knight and courtly love to a grander Christian narrative.

Rereading the story recently, I was struck by a scene that seems inexplicably cruel: Having tamed the dragon so that it is no longer a threat, George offers to decapitate it if all the townspeople adopt his religion. After some twenty thousand pagans convert to Christianity, he indeed beheads the dragon. The monster, we're to believe, is no longer dangerous, and so its death is offered as part of a distasteful bargain: *Pledge your soul to my religion, and I'll satisfy your bloodlust and your need for revenge.* George was fast becoming, like Foy, a violent saint. Of course you could argue that any military saint, including Barbara, dealt in violence, but Barbara you called on to keep you from harm. George was the saint you took to war.

England's Edward I took George along when he invaded Wales in 1277. He adopted George as his patron for two reasons: first because he was eager to justify his conquest as a holy crusade. Second, and even more to the point, Wales had long adopted the dragon as its own symbol, and Edward's invocation of George helped to transform an image of strength into a symbol of evil. Edward prevailed as George had over the dragon, bringing English law to Wales, which was in time incorporated into what became the United Kingdom. In the process, the English sought to bring homogeneity to their island, erasing any cultural, linguistic, or national differences. The warrior-saint, George, now a national symbol, became inherently bound up in national conquest, in colonization.

Later kings Edward III and Henry V also invoked George as their protector, and the relative success of these three monarchs helped to establish the saint's iconic status as the patron of England. When the fiercely anti-Catholic Edmund Spenser wrote his epic in honor of Queen Elizabeth, *The Faerie Queene*, he began with George—though he could not, of course, call him that. Instead, George is stripped of his Catholicism and rechristened "the Redcrosse Knight" (after George's famous red cross on a white background, which became England's flag). Spenser's hatred of Catholicism went beyond matters of doctrine: Like many

Anglicans, he despised the proliferation of "idolatrous" artwork and decoration in the Catholic Church, and so the Redcrosse Knight's supreme antagonist is named Arch-Imago, the "Great Image." Spenser was equally suspicious of the writings of the Catholic fathers, which is why the first beast Redcrosse slays, Error, vomits "bookes and papers" along with "loathly frogs and toades." By Spenser's reckoning, a disguised George now wages war against Jerome and Gregory the Great, as Elizabeth was engaged in purging England of Catholics.

It may seem odd that in critiquing the Catholic Church, Spenser used as his champion one of its most famous saints, but the warrior-knight has always had shifting allegiances. The obscurity of his origins have given him a fluidity to be whatever he is needed to be: Now he gives birth to monsters, now he fights against them, now for Catholicism and now against it. It seems as if the sword of George, a holy mercenary, is always for hire.

As a saint without fixed loyalty, George is free to represent all things to all people. The crusaders may have taken him with them back to Europe, but of course he also remained a presence in the Middle East. As a result, George's legend evolved in two different strands. In England, he's become the crusader knight, the slayer of dragons; in the Middle East, he is still the agricultural patron who brings good crops and healthy livestock and is particularly helpful in matters of fertility.

English Protestants like Spenser were perfectly comfortable calling on George as their patron, but then, so were members of other religions. That is, as the Middle East continued to evolve over the centuries, Islam gradually displacing Christianity, George didn't disappear; he instead became one of those exceedingly rare figures: an interfaith saint. Muslims came to know him as Khidr, "the Green One," affording him the same respect as did the remaining Christians, and now in the Middle East, both Muslims and Christians come to pray at his shrine.

In the town of Beit Jala, outside Bethlehem, is a chapel devoted to George, a shrine that has long been used as a makeshift insane asylum. According J. E. Hannauer's *Folklore of the Holy Land: Muslim, Christian, and Jewish*, published in 1907, George's shrine is described as a "sort of madhouse. Deranged persons of all three faiths are taken thither and chained in the court of the chapel, where they are kept for forty days on bread and water, the Greek priest at the head of the establishment now and then reading the Gospel over them, or administering a whipping as the case demands." Although this practice has been discontinued in the hundred years since, one can still speak of someone going mad as "going to St. George's."

When William Dalrymple visited George's shrine in the 1990s, the Greek Orthodox priest who ran the shrine complained of hundreds of Muslim pilgrims, "all over the floor, in the aisles, up and down . . . bottoms in the air, prayer mats on the floor: yes—in an Orthodox church!" They brought prayer mats adorned with images of Mecca to show their devotion to George-Khidr and told Dalrymple of miraculous sightings of him on his white horse, performing miracles for the faithful and unconcerned by which faith they might represent.

It is odd that a saint who is so strongly associated with nationalism and conquest, with the obliteration of monsters and of other cultures, should also be a symbol of heterogeneity and contradiction, his shrine a place where devout Muslims leave tokens of gratitude for Greek Orthodox priests. One is left wondering if George, for all his chivalric virtue, is himself a monster of conflicting ideas and beliefs—as if the dragon he's fighting is also himself.

FIFTEEN

In the Darkest Nights
of the Year: Lucy

Van Gogh's *The Night Café* is an image of destitution, its garish colors unable to hide its bleak desperation. Around the edges of the room huddle silent patrons, beneath the dandelion-halos of a few harsh overhead lights. The painting's perspective is skewed: A billiards table juts out at an improbable angle, and the floor tilts forward as if the whole room is ready to spill onto the ground at the viewer's feet. It's an unsettling image, a distorted view through diseased eyes, vertiginous and bleak. "I have tried to express the idea that the café is a place where one can ruin oneself, go mad or commit a crime," Van Gogh wrote to his brother Theo. "So I have tried to express, as it were, the powers of darkness in a low public house, by soft Louis XV green and malachite, contrasting with yellow-green and harsh blue-greens, and all this in an atmosphere like a devil's furnace, of pale sulphur. And all with an appearance of Japanese gaiety, and the good nature of Tartarin." Van Gogh sought to unearth the darkness in something as banal as an all-night bar to show us what's hiding underneath.

A month after Van Gogh finished *The Night Café*, Paul Gauguin arrived in Arles, invited by the younger painter to form something like an artist's colony in a small yellow house where Van Gogh had been living. Gauguin arrived at night, waiting until daybreak at the same all-night café, that place of infernal solitude. Things did not go well; within a few weeks, their relationship had begun to sour. "Gauguin," Van Gogh wrote to his brother, "does not like the little yellow cottage." They quarreled about art, and about money. ("One thing that made him angry was having to acknowledge that I was very intelligent," Gauguin later wrote with characteristic humility.) Even as they painted each other's portraits and encouraged each other's work, Van Gogh's behavior became increasingly erratic, and a few times Gauguin awoke in the dead of night to find Van Gogh standing directly over his bed, silently staring at him.

Just after the winter solstice, on one of the darkest nights of the year, Van Gogh ended an argument by flinging a glass of absinthe at Gauguin's face, and the latter resolved to leave Arles for good. The next night—December 23—Gauguin was walking home when, as he later recalled, "I heard a well-known little step behind me, quick and jerky. I turned around just as Vincent rushed at me with an open razor in his hand." Van Gogh halted abruptly, and in that bleak alleyway the two men stared at each other for a long, perhaps interminable, moment. "The look in my eyes at that moment must have been very powerful," Gauguin wrote, "for he stopped, lowered his head and ran back toward the house."

Van Gogh took Luke the Evangelist as his patron because Luke is the saint of painters. But the saint whom I most associate with this artist, and particularly with that dead winter night in Arles, is not Luke but Lucy, patron of the darkest nights of the year. Lucy's story began as a sort of sequel to that of another saint—as a young girl she'd come to pray at Agatha's shrine, bringing along her mother, hoping to cure her dysentery. Agatha not only cured Lucy's mother but also appeared to the young girl in a vision, telling her that she, too, would one day be revered in her home of Syracuse as Agatha was in Catania. Lucy, like Agatha, subsequently pledged her virginity and paid a similarly high price for it—she, too, was sent to a brothel at one point and later tortured. And, like Agatha, she's now recognized by the body part cut from her during these tortures: her eyes.

At least, that's the most common version of Lucy's story; there are differing accounts of how she lost her eyes. Another involves a suitor who relentlessly pursued the virginal Lucy, repeatedly complimenting her on the beauty of her eyes. Lucy, wanting to be left in peace, simply gouged out her eyes and sent them to the suitor, telling him he was free to have them if he felt they were so beautiful and asking to be finally left in peace.

This story is likely apocryphal, but it has echoes of another, a story that also happened on December 23, 1888. After threatening Gauguin with a straight razor, Van Gogh took that same razor to a nearby brothel, where he cut off a portion of his right earlobe, giving it to a prostitute named Rachel and asking her to hold it for safekeeping.

It was these dual stories of self-mutilation that initially led me to equate Van Gogh and Lucy, but there are other reasons why I think he should have adopted her over Luke. "The symbol of St. Luke, the patron saint of painters, is, as you know, an ox," Van Gogh wrote to Émile Bernard in the summer of 1888. "So you just be patient as an ox if you want to work in the artistic field." But Van Gogh didn't need a patron saint of patience; he needed a saint of the night, when he was most troubled. ("The thing I *dread* most is insomnia," he wrote to his brother after he'd been hospitalized.) He needed a saint to offer hope in the darkness, salvation from the darkness of winter.

The details of Van Gogh's self-mutilation remain murky, in no small part because the primary account of the event comes from Gauguin, hardly a reliable source. But, then, it is hard to understand self-mutilation at all. What must Lucy's act have looked like? Was it slow, grinding, bloody work as she grunted and moaned, working the knife? Or was she hardly conscious of it, distracted by her own sublimity, perhaps humming?

Figure 12: Statue of Saint Lucy, Saint Roch's Cemetery,
New Orleans © Joanna Ebenstein

I imagine that no one but I thinks much about the specifics of Lucy's gouging out her own eyes, even though this is what makes her the saint she is. Yet I'll confess that I have trouble *not* thinking about the particularities of the event, even supposing it's apocryphal. Many saints are defined almost exclusively by their bodies, by what they did with them and what was done to them. And yet their bodies are what we cannot or will not face. In Lucy's act hide these paradoxes of devotion, complications of faith, and the body we'd rather not see. Earlier audiences, I think, would not have overly troubled themselves with questions as to the details of such a horrific moment. One's own time and place, I suppose, greatly influence how one feels about the bodies of the saints and the degree to which one seeks to understand those bodies.

D ante Alighieri, for one, didn't seem too concerned with the body of a saint like Lucy. Like Van Gogh, he was half mad, wandering through a desolate forest in the middle of the night when Lucy found him in need of salvation. Lucy plays a key role in the *Divine Comedy*; alerted to Dante's presence by the Virgin Mary, Lucy turns to Beatrice to aid this pilgrim through the perilous night:

> Beatrice, true praise of God,
> why do you not help the one who loved you so
> that for your sake he left the vulgar herd?

Do you not hear the anguish in his tears?
do you not see the death besetting him
on the swollen river where the sea cannot prevail?

The Dante scholar Robert Hollander notes of these lines, "As tormented a passage as may be found in this canto, and one of the most difficult in the entire work." Readers of Dante have spent a great deal of time puzzling out that swollen river, that sea—it seems a metaphorical death besetting him; perhaps he is wasting away from love of Beatrice. But what an odd image, where the swollen river is that figure of death while the sea is salvation.

Dante's Lucy often calls attention to her own eyes. In *Purgatorio*, Canto IX, it is Lucy who picks up the sleeping Dante and carries him to the gate of Purgatory to begin his ascent. "Here she set you down," Virgil tells him, "but first her lovely eyes showed me that entrance, standing open." It is Lucy's lovely eyes, her *occhi belli*, that guide our hero, who does not pause to mention the stories of the violent fate that befell such beautiful eyes. For Dante, Lucy's power and her life could be contained in her name alone, from the Latin *lux*, "light." Scholars have even suggested that these stories about her mutilated eyes were created years after Dante; it was not until the Middle Ages, some have argued, that she became known as the patron saint of blindness, bearing those startling eyes on her tray. Lucy's story, perhaps, evolved simply from the meaning of her name, like Foy's. And like Foy, it may be that she was originally less a person than an ideal, a symbol.

Which would have suited Dante; his poetry described a symbolic world rather than one of flesh and blood. In Dante's world, criminals are punished and saints rewarded, but all not only according to justice but also according to a poetic and symbolic system. When he wrote of Lucy, he wrote in careful, beautiful verse, an explanation of a pure, ordered world in which each creature and object and saint was in its right place. Lucy, patron of lucidity, of a clear picture of the world even in the darkness, perhaps best exemplifies this. John Freccero contends that "the purpose of the entire journey is to write the poem, to attain the vantage-point of Lucy," from which Dante hopes to perceive "the coherence in life, and to bear witness to that coherence for other men." But while this may be true, the splendor of Dante's great opus may also simply be a ward against a deeper fear, that there was nothing but suffering, nothing but Chaos, the mother of Night.

Dante's poem takes place over Easter, but Lucy's time is the winter, when the nights are long and unforgiving. Midwinter is sometimes called the "days of roughness," precisely because it was impossible for earlier cultures to identify that exact moment when the earth begins its tilt back. Lucy, patron saint of blindness and of the darkest nights of the year, is meant to be celebrated on the solstice itself, but pinpointing the exact moment of the solstice has never been easy. Her feast day was originally on December 16, though it later changed to December 13. Neither of these is close to the solstice as we now understand it, but prior to the Gregorian calendar, the date of the solstice changed every hundred years. The Julian calendar was based on a calculation of 365.25 days to a year, when in fact the number is closer to 365.2422, creating a slight slippage that had added up to thirteen full days before Pope Gregory XII rectified it in 1582.

Lucy's day was still December 16 when Dante wrote his epic in the early 1300s, though the solstice then would have fallen on December 12. When John Donne took Lucy as his muse three hundred years later, the longest night of the year was December 9. But Donne's great poem to Lucy, "A Nocturnal upon Saint Lucy's Day, Being the Shortest Day," is dated December 7. Donne didn't know when the solstice occurred, nor when Lucy's actual feast day was, but he understood on some level that Lucy's is a movable feast—her day is every night, since at night all calendars stop.

> Study me then, you who shall lovers be
> At the next world, that is, at the next spring;
> For I am every dead thing,
> In whom Love wrought new alchemy.

Donne was far less sanguine than Dante that the world is perfectly ordered and just. He had been born Catholic in a newly Protestant country, which was being torn apart by religion and by conflicting views of the order of the world. His brother Henry was imprisoned in 1593 for harboring a Catholic priest and died of disease in prison (the priest, meanwhile, had been hanged until he was nearly dead, at which point he was disemboweled). Donne had learned to keep his faith a secret throughout his early years before ultimately converting to the Anglican faith in 1627.

It was three years later, with the deaths of both his patron, Countess Lucy of Bedford, and his young daughter Lucy, that Donne turned to the Catholic saint of darkness. Like Dante, he came to Lucy in his darkest hour, beset by gloom. But unlike the Italian, Donne could not find solace in a divinely revealed master plan of the universe. Dante found a love beyond death through Lucy's intercession, but Donne saw death hidden even in love, despair that outweighed belief, darkness to match the longest night of the year. The bleakness of Donne's work dispels the order in Dante. If the Italian found paradise emerging from the inferno, Donne found midnight in a summer's kiss. "I am re-begot," he tells us, "Of absence, darkness, death—things which are not." Donne called on Lucy in the wake of a personal loss, and his poem suggests that if God exists, His purpose is only to affirm our emptiness. Lucy's name is here invoked to remind Donne that the world will yet turn back on its axis, even if Donne himself can't yet see it.

V an Gogh might have been the third of Lucy's most famous acolytes, *The Night Café* seen as the final panel in a triptych. But he could not make it through the darkness, nor could he find Lucy waiting in the gloom. A shame. To Dante's certainty and

Donne's gloom Lucy could have added Van Gogh's madness, carnivalesque in its motley, a fluorescent night of death. Lucy could have seen through the dark streets of Arles and the harsh glare of the Night Café, which was, after all, just one more inferno to be navigated. All of us, at one time or another in our lives, must follow Lucy, even if we don't call to her out loud.

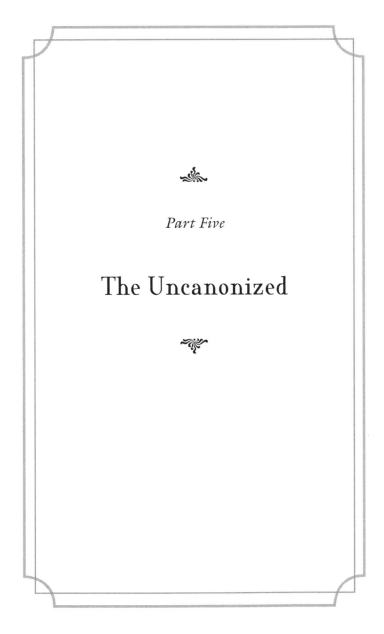

Part Five

The Uncanonized

·SIXTEEN·

The Consolations of
Castration: Origen

As strange as the stories of the saints are the stories at the
margins of sainthood, the men and women who might have
been saints but somehow failed to make the cut, those who lived
their devotion but died in obscurity or ignominy. They are perhaps even more beautiful because of their failure, the ones who
wagered all and were repaid with apathy—or, in the case of the
third-century theologian Origen, were held up repeatedly as an
example of error. I first learned briefly of Origen while in Catholic
school; a powerful mind and a major figure of the early church,
once mentioned in the same breath as Augustine and Jerome, he
was brought up as an aside and quickly dismissed. Despite the
sway he once held, his legacy has been largely forgotten or actively

suppressed. Within the grand narrative of the church, there is now not much to be said about him at all.

So to tell Origen's story well, one must start earlier—before his birth, before Christ, before everything, even time itself—with a simple love story. It goes like this: A man and a woman love each other very much; there is nothing in the world but the two of them. The man loves the woman so much, in fact, that he's terrified of anything that could ever come between them. His love for her is so all-encompassing that he begins to dread the thought of children, of children who he thinks will divide the two of them. He loathes the thought of his own offspring, even though he cannot keep her from getting pregnant.

This man has reason to fear their children, after all. When they come, they are monstrous, so unspeakably hideous that he cannot stand the sight of them, so horrific that they defy description.

Finally he solves his problem. When his wife gives birth, he simply shoves the child back into her womb. One by one, he takes his awful progeny and crams them back up the birth canal, as if to undo the atrocity of their birth. To keep these monsters inside the womb of their mother, he decides simply never to pull out; he plugs her birth canal with his penis, blocking his offspring's entrance into the world.

It is an intolerable situation, and it cannot last. Finally this woman, unable to bear the pain of so many monsters trapped inside her, devises a plan; she gives one of her children—the smartest, the most bold—a sickle, and he acts. He castrates his father, freeing the children's escape route and ending the tyranny of the father once and for all.

This is how the love affair ends; and how the woman, Gaia, the earth, becomes separated from Uranus, the sky; and how their son, Chronos, his wife and sister, Rhea, and the Titans finally enter the world. This is the birth of chronology, the end of prehistory, and the beginning of time.

In Greek mythology, castration makes the world. Castration sets everything in motion; it creates love, it creates beauty, it creates justice. The blood dripping from Uranus's penis spills on the ground, and from these drops of blood are born the Furies, who dispense justice, as well as the Giants and the Nymphs of the Ash Tree. Then Chronos tosses his father's penis into the sea, and when it touches the sea foam, Aphrodite is born—the goddess of love, born of castration and the sea.

From Aphrodite comes a second great love story, this one in the very real time of the twelfth century and the very real place of Paris. There, possessed by Aphrodite, by love and desire and lust, a young and promising theologian seduced a young woman he had been tutoring, impregnating her. When her uncle learned of this, the theologian agreed to marry her, but after their son's birth, he had her sent to a convent, and her uncle, believing she had been abandoned and ruined, sent thugs to this young man while he was sleeping and had him castrated. This is the story of Heloïse and Abelard.

Castration made Abelard, as it made Heloïse. Abelard was a rising scholar, one of the greatest minds of medieval Europe, but only after his castration, only after he was permanently separated from Heloïse, only after the two of them began writing letters to each other did their story achieve immortality. Now their story was tragic, and in time their names would be said alongside those of Tristan and Isolde, Romeo and Juliet—a love triumphant in spite of, and because of, castration.

In his misery, Abelard turned to the story of Origen for comfort. Abelard had already been compared to Origen for his rhetorical brilliance, his ability to use the profane arts of secular literature and culture "as a hook, baited with a taste of philosophy, to draw listeners towards the study of the true philosophy." But now he had another thing in common with Origen because Origen is the patron saint of the castrated.

Origen's story, too, is a love story in which he is in love with Christ, in which he is the bride of Christ. Origen strove to be perfect, without sin or distraction. He read Jesus's words in Matthew 19:12: "There be eunuchs, which have made themselves eunuchs for the kingdom of heaven's sake," and in Matthew 18:9: "If thine eye offend thee, pluck it out, and cast it from thee; it is better for thee to enter into life with one eye, rather than having two eyes and be cast into hell." Origen had an unrivaled intellect but eventually started to feel that his own biological urges might distract him from a full dedication to God, and so, offended by his own sex, he castrated himself.

The Uncanonized

⁂

Castration looms large in the history of Christianity, but nowhere as large as in Russia. It was there, in 1771, that a local prefect arrested a man named Andrei Ivanov for persuading thirteen other men to castrate themselves. Ivanov was knouted—that is, whipped with a special cat-o'-nine-tails tipped with metal rings and hooks—and then sent into Siberia. But his assistant, Kondratii Selivanov, managed to flee and soon set up shop in Saint Petersburg as the returned Christ, the lord of castration.

Selivanov's teaching was simple. After Adam and Eve had eaten the apple but before they were expelled from the Garden, they had cut the apple in half and grafted it onto their bodies. A woman's breasts and a man's genitals were the literal remnant of this sin, protuberances not natural to the human body, the markers of our transgression and the key to our salvation. If the Greeks saw castration at the beginning of time, the Skoptsy cult (the word means simply "eunuch") that followed Selivanov saw castration as the means to heal the wound at the beginning of time. Castration was no longer just generative; now it was also regenerative, redemptive.

The Skoptsy cult quickly seized Russia in the nineteenth century. There was the "lesser seal," the removal of one's testicles, and the "greater seal," which included the removal of the penis as well—or, in the case of a woman, a double mastectomy. This was the only means to purity for the Skoptsy, who also called them-selves "the White Doves."

What started as a movement among illiterate peasants quickly grew to include nobility, merchants, and clergy, even after Kondratii Selivanov's imprisonment and eventual death in 1832. The government tried to crush the sect by deporting over seven hundred Skoptsy to Siberia in the middle of the century, but the movement continued to grow: By 1874, there were close to six thousand members, over eight hundred of whom had received their greater or lesser seals.

The Skoptsy were apocalyptic; they believed that when their numbers reached 144,000, the Messiah would return to earth. Theirs was a castration to heal the world, castration to end the world. While they waited, they continued to populate the world; at their height, they estimated close to 100,000 members. The Romanian writer I. L. Caragiale quipped that in turn-of-the-century Bucharest, every horse-drawn carriage was driven by Skoptsy who had fled the persecutions in Russia. In *Kaputt*, his bleak dispatch from the wastelands of Eastern Europe during World War II, the Italian ex-fascist Curzio Malaparte described a Skoptsy in a similar role, a coachman for a sadistic Moldavian princess, prepared to destroy a shopkeeper over a bag of tea. This description was one of the first times I had read of the Skoptsy, though years before, I had seen the skull of a former cult member on display in the Mütter Museum in Philadelphia. Malaparte's description of the driver raising a whip toward the miserable shopkeeper, "lifting and stretching his arms as if he were holding a flagpole in his fist," helped cement in me the image of the Skoptsy as otherworldly, greater or lesser than human, a sign of the end of the world to be sure.

We may never know whether castration would have brought about the end of the world as it brought about the beginning, since the Soviets thoroughly crushed the Skoptsy movement, which died out sometime in the middle of the twentieth century. Malaparte's driver, in fact, may have been among the last of the dying sect. But modern psychiatric literature includes a diagnosis of Skoptsy syndrome, a desire to castrate oneself. Indeed, a Philadelphia urologist has recently claimed to have performed over twelve thousand voluntary castrations at his practice.

If Origen had no literal offspring, he can still claim these White Doves as his children. Castration has its own consolations. What troubled both Origen and the Skoptsy is the eternal problem of Christian genitals—if they're the root of sin, then isn't their removal a possible path to purity?

Origen's name appears regularly as one of the four theological titans of the early Christian church, with Augustine, Ambrose, and Jerome. But of the four, only Origen was never made a saint by the church. Considering what he's contributed to doctrine, this seems somehow unjust. Most commentators agree that Origen was denied sainthood for a few ideas later deemed heretical: his belief in the preexistence of souls, for example, in which he went so far as to claim that even devils—even Satan himself—had immortal souls. His castration alone might not have been enough to bar him from sainthood, but it clings to him anyway, a persistent stain on his character and further evidence of his wrongheaded approach to theology. Particularly now, when those early theological debates have long since faded from all but the most esoteric memories, Origen is remembered not as the heretic but as the castrated one.

Other saints mutilated themselves, including (supposedly) Lucy. But then, eyes are not testicles. And though it may be better to enter the kingdom blind than in sin, castration really is something altogether different. Leviticus 22:24 warns, "Ye shall not present to the Lord any animal if its testicles have been bruised, or crushed, torn or cut." And Deuteronomy 23:1 pointedly proclaims, "No man whose testicles have been crushed or whose organ has been severed shall become a member of the assembly of the Lord." Of all the bodily mutilations one can suffer, castration is the most taboo. The word *unmanned* has this other definition: The eunuch is no longer a member of the human community. Abelard, after all, was a rising figure in the church, but after he was unmanned, he was forced to leave the clergy. One cannot testify without one's testicles.

But, as in many areas of doctrine, it turns out that the attitude of the church on this matter isn't quite so simple. "Let women keep silent in church," Paul says in First Corinthians, 14:34. And so church fathers who wanted the beauty of a soprano voice to say mass had to find other means. Starting around the Renaissance, a new solution was devised: A boy with a promising voice would be

taken to a bath infused with herbs and given opiates or asphyxi-
ated so as to numb the pain of what was about to happen. Then
someone would reach in and brutally massage his genitals until
the testicles were crushed; eventually they would dissolve and be
reabsorbed by the body.

Without testosterone, the body changes—the bone joints do
not harden, and so the bones grow long and thin; the limbs elon-
gate along with the ribs, creating an increased lung capacity. This,
along with underdeveloped vocal cords, gives a castrato an incredible range and an otherworldly voice. A castrato is not just a soprano but an unreal figure, unmanned, ethereal, somehow more
than human.

Castrati were enormously popular, and their fame lasted for
three centuries. Operas were written for them and about them,
and every major church choir was populated with them. Their decline was due less to ethics than to taste and a rise in the popularity
of tenors in the mid–nineteenth century. Though castrati were finally outlawed in Italy in 1870, the Sistine Choir still had them as
late as 1903.

Modern church history, then, is oddly intertwined with castration. The same prohibition in Leviticus that kept Abelard out
of the church was trumped, two centuries later, by a Bible verse
that brought in the castrati. So I find myself returning to this
question: Was castration truly the horrible fate that kept Origen
out of the pantheon of saints? Certainly Abelard didn't think so.
In his second letter to Heloïse, he mentions Origen as his brother
in emasculation but goes on to suggest that Origen's problem was

not castration but poor interpretation of the Scriptures. "The great Christian philosopher Origen," he writes,

> was not afraid to mutilate himself in order to quench completely this fire within him, as if he understood literally the words that those men were truly blessed who castrated themselves for the Kingdom of Heaven's sake, and believed them to be truthfully carrying out the bidding of the Lord about offending members, that we should cut them off and throw them away; and as if he interpreted as historic fact, not as hidden symbol, that prophecy of Isaiah in which the Lord prefers eunuchs to the rest of the faithful.

Abelard needs to believe that he himself, castrated against his will, can still be saved, even though Origen was not. And so it is Origen's inability to distinguish the hidden symbol from the historical fact that creates a problem in Abelard's eyes. To be castrated is unfortunate but not fatal; rather, the great sin of Origen, like that of the Skoptsy, is taking things too literally, not understanding how metaphor works.

But Origen's sin is more than just an overly literal reading, just as it is more than a literal castration. Origen's sin is greater and less than metaphor, just as castration is greater and less than sin. Castration, maker of the world and harbinger of its end, the father of those men who have become greater and less than human.

SEVENTEEN

At the Well of Tears:
Margery Kempe

"Tears did not enter the world through the saints; but without them we would have never known that we cry because we long for a lost paradise." So wrote the Romanian philosopher E. M. Cioran, whose nihilism and atheism didn't stop him from approaching the saints. "As I searched for tears," he tells us, "I thought of the saints." The two are inextricably linked: weeping and sainthood. Despite the various stories and legends, the transcendent artwork and architecture and literary masterpieces, perhaps it is only in tears that we can really hope to understand the saints.

More than laughter, mourning, or sex, crying (which can encompass all of these things) is the truly excessive gesture, the limit of emotion available to us. If the saint, as I want to believe, is the human who lives poised at the edge of humanity—who might even move beyond humanity—then weeping is the act that most closely corresponds with this position. "Saints cannot be *known*," Cioran says. "Only when we awaken the tears sleeping in our depths and know *through* them, do we come to understand how someone could renounce being a man." Only humans, out of all animals, cry, but only in weeping, Cioran seems to be saying, do we transcend our humanity.

Tears have long fascinated the church. Gregory the Great first coined the term *gratia lachrimarum*, which can mean either "the tears of grace" or "the gift of tears," as though to be moved to tears is a gift given by God to evidence our own salvation. The fifth-century desert hermit Abbot Isaac tried to make a taxonomy of wordless Christian weeping, classifying four kinds: tears caused by "the pricks of sin smiting our heart," tears "from contemplation of eternal good and desire of that further glory," tears from a fear of the day of Judgment, and tears caused by the knowledge of the sins of others. All of the saints, in one way or another, sought such tears; Saint Francis, it is said, wept so much that he went blind.

One woman among the saints wept more copiously, more spectacularly, than anyone before her or since. Her name was Margery Kempe, of Lynn, England. She was a middle-class wife and mother of fourteen children who was born sometime in the

1370s and lived until the middle of the next century. Margery had been a brewer and a miller and had held a half-dozen other occupations when, in the middle of her life, Jesus appeared to her fully and radically.

And then she began to weep, a torrent of tears that never stopped. You cannot open her autobiography anywhere without stumbling on a passage of her weeping; it saturates the text. Most often, it seems that her tears fall into the first of Abbot Isaac's categories: Beholding her own wickedness, Margery "sorrows and weeps and prays for mercy and forgiveness." She wept the third kind of tears at the thought of her own damnation until Jesus appeared to her and assured her of her salvation, and then she wept the second kind of tears instead.

Margery became a holy pilgrim, traveling among the various communities in rural England and on to Canterbury, then London. In London, she began to build a following as more and more people gathered to hear the weeping woman—"her communication was so much of the love of God that the hearers were oftentimes stirred through it to weep right soberly." From there, she went to Julian of Norwich, the mystic anchoress, and then to Jerusalem and Rome. An endless wanderer, she stayed among monks and in convents, sometimes with her husband, sometimes without. All the while crying.

She wept copiously, profusely, bitterly, loudly, ecstatically, endlessly. She was a torrent of tears. She wept at sermons, at the mention of Christ's Passion, or whenever the Holy Ghost moved her. In the Church of Saint John Laterne, she "wept bitterly, she sobbed violently, and cried full loudly." There is a struggle for more words to name this phenomenon, words beyond "wept," "sobbed," "cried," words that appear hundreds of times throughout the book. She wept so much while staying in an abbey in Canterbury that the monks would not let her eat in their presence. Her weeping drove away a traveling companion in Germany, and in Rome, she wept so bitterly that the congregants around her thought her possessed. While staying with the priests of Saint Thomas of Canterbury, she wept so much that the head of the order kicked her out, and then she wept the fourth kind of tears at the thought of his callousness and wickedness.

Weeping was Margery's vocation. "It is a singular and a special gift that God has given you," Jerome told her in a vision, "a well of tears which man shall never take from you." In another vision, Jesus told her it was her lot to weep, unceasingly, for fifteen years.

When she was not weeping, she performed her share of miracles—her prayers interceding on behalf of those at the edge of death. How many she saved isn't clear—"to write them all should perhaps be a hindrance to more profit," she tells us, cutting herself off. Besides, Margery's real miracle is her tears, the endless torrent of weeping, as though she invented her own language of wordless moaning. Margery's autobiography is a book of tears, and she ends it with a defense of her crying:

As for my crying, sobbing, and my weeping, Lord God almighty, as surely as you know what scorns, what shames, what despites, and what reproofs I have had for it, and, as surely as it is not in my power to weep either loud or still for any devotion nor for any sweetness but only through the gift of the Holy Ghost, so surely, Lord, excuse me before all this world.

And yet, she was not a saint.

The process of canonization is long, resembling a court proceeding more than an intervention by God. Petitioners may recommend a candidate as a "Servant of God" no sooner than five years after death, and after the local bishop reviews extensive documentation and confirms that the candidate is not the focus of a cult or other heretical worship, the congregation petitions the pope to elevate the candidate to "venerable." The next step beyond venerable is beatified; though this state is easily achieved in the case of martyrdom, nonmartyrs have to perform at least one after-death miracle, which is rigorously investigated by the church. A second miracle is required, ultimately, for full canonization.

Lengthy, but in its own way fairly straightforward. The reasons Margery has never been canonized are painfully obvious. She was already a married woman, with children, when Christ came to her fully, so she could not be his virgin bride. She could have retired to a convent but chose not to do so, nor did she subordinate herself under a powerful male protector, as many other female saints (including Teresa of Avila) did. She chose instead to remain her own person, to wander, to cause trouble. None of her children worked very hard to keep her name alive or spread tales of her miracles, and certainly the various hospices and monasteries along the road to Jerusalem were glad to be rid of her.

There was no one to advocate on Margery's behalf, which is what is truly involved in achieving sainthood. More than performing miracles or crying over the Passion of Christ, canonization requires a community to believe in you after your death; it requires that you be kept alive in the minds of those you leave behind.

The church was wrong to canonize so few women saints," Cioran argues. "Its misogyny and stinginess make me want to be more generous. Any woman who sheds tears for love in loneliness is a saint. The Church has never understood that saintly women are made of God's tears." The church's official position is that it does not "make" saints; it only recognizes and affirms the saints already among us. It falls to God to designate the saints, and so, the church might respond, it is God's stinginess, God's misogyny, that has provided for so few women saints.

Certainly this accords with the long-standing popular belief that men are closer to God than are women—"him to love God, her to love God in him," Milton writes in *Paradise Lost*, apportioning out the spiritual roles of Adam and Eve. Medieval Christian theologians took justification for their misogyny in part from Aristotle, who argued that semen was "frothy," composed of water and *pneuma*, hot vapor (this, so he claims, is why semen does not freeze)—it is the hot vapor that contains and transmits the soul. This hierarchy of bodily fluids held throughout the medieval Christian world. Men were closer to God, as evidenced by the hot vapor in their semen, whereas menstrual blood was pure water— no froth there, no air inside the woman, who was far more earthly, somewhat lacking in soul. In 1579, the French physiologist Laurent Joubert noted that "weeping is easier for those weaker and moister." So perhaps Margery's copious tears guaranteed that she would never be a saint—there was too much water in her, too little air.

Or perhaps she spent too much time weeping in public. Augustine, after all, held back tears at his mother's funeral, fearing that a public display would show him "guilty of too much worldly affection," offering his sincere tears to God only in private. Margery's tears were too public, her emotion indecorously shoved in the faces of the faithful. Her weeping was never the quiet, demure crying of a good lady martyr. She did not yoke herself to a powerful male figure, and she did not die pure. After her death, her body did not lie uncorrupted, proof of her pure negation of the natural world. Margery could not make of herself a symbol.

Samuel Beckett once wrote, "My words are my tears." Margery Kempe, finally exhausted by tears, turned to words and traded the immortal life of a saint for the immortal life of a writer.

It was perhaps because she feared she would never be canonized that she did so. Her autobiography became a substitute for the hagiography that would never be. Hers is as compelling and strange a story as one could hope—and the first autobiography written in English. In it, she never calls herself "I" but always "this creature": "Then this creature thought it was full merry to be reproved for God's love"; "this creature dared not otherwise to do than she was commanded in her soul"; and so on, distancing us from her even while drawing us in.

This creature turns out to be surprisingly frank about her sexuality, with regard to both her husband and her lovers. After she stopped sleeping with her husband, he began tormenting her with hypothetical questions: If someone threatened to cut off his head unless she slept with him once more, he asked, would she do it? Margery's response was blunt: "I had rather see you be slain than we should turn again to our uncleanness."

But around the same time, she began an affair with a brute of a man who told her "he would lie by her and have his lust of his body, and she should not withstand him, for, if he might not have his will that time, he said, he should else have it another time, she could not choose." After he'd satisfied himself, this creature returned to him, infatuated and still "labored" with him, only to be told that "he wouldn't for all the good in this world" lie with her again, that "he had rather been hewn as small as meat for the pot." A strange way to begin the autobiography of a holy woman, with infidelity compounded by a fairly pathetic rejection.

All this was before her great conversion, and before all the weeping, but it's still too much information for a would-be saint. Margery's autobiography is too messy, too candid, and it could never guarantee that she would be remembered. Her book was quickly lost and forgotten as this would-be weeping saint faded from sight.

Then, in 1934, the autobiography was rediscovered and brought to the public eye once more. It should have been the perfect time for Margery's voice to reemerge; Virginia Woolf had opened up new possibilities for writing women's consciousness only a decade before, and Djuna Barnes's *Nightwood* was only two years away. Instead, Margery's writing was met with derision, particularly its representation of so much uncontrolled emotion in a woman. She was denounced as a "terrible hysteric," a "neurotic," "quite mad," an "epileptic," with "a large paranoid trend," and all sorts of other epithets. Margery could have expected this; in one of her earliest visions, she heard Christ tell her, "You shall be eaten and gnawed by the people as any rat gnaws the stockfish." It hardly matters, then, if the rats gnawing at her were fifteenth-century monks or twentieth-century psychoanalysts.

"Sometimes one meets a woman who is beast turning human," Djuna Barnes writes. In our new century, though, one sees in Margery a beast that is woman becoming saint. Slowly, in the decades since her rediscovery, she has found her admirers. "She replaced existence with the desire to exist," Robert Glück explains in his book *Margery Kempe*, which weaves her story alongside his narrative of a contemporary love affair. "I kept Margery in mind for twenty-five years," he writes, "but couldn't enter her love until I also loved a young man who was above me." Margery's love is difficult, uncompromising, but readers and writers like Glück keep finding her, finding kinship with that love in an equally impossible contemporary landscape. A community of believers, the wasted and the hopeful, the freaks and the dreamers, gradually grows around her. Perhaps sainthood will find her yet.

Notes on Sources

PROLOGUE

The Buñuel quotes are from *My Last Sigh* and *An Unspeakable Betrayal*; the Michael Wood essay on Buñuel's *Simon of the Desert* can be found in the Criterion Collection booklet accompanying the film. The Mary Gordon interview aired on *Fresh Air* with Terry Gross on January 31, 2005. Kenzaburo Oë's recollections of childhood are discussed in John Nathan's introduction to Oë's *Teach Us to Outgrow Our Madness*. My discussion of plagiarism and hagiography benefits from an aside in Carolyn Dinshaw's *Chaucer's Sexual Poetics*.

PART ONE

The translation I used for Gregory of Tours's work is by Lewis Thorpe. Hayden White's thoughts on history are from the essay "The Value of Narrativity in the Representation of Reality," in W. J. T. Mitchell's anthology *On Narrative*. Frank Kermode's words come from his *A Sense of an Ending: Studies in the Theory of Fiction*. The translation of Borges's

"The Library of Babel" is Andrew Hurley's; his comment on Leibniz comes from *Seven Nights*. My understanding of Chaucer and the role of dreaming in his books owes a debt to Piero Boitani's essay in *The Cambridge Companion to Chaucer*, and the scholar who suggests that his work is an attempt to imagine himself in the position of a woman is Carolyn Dinshaw. The translation of *Hekabe* I used is by Anne Carson, from her *Grief Lessons*. Radegund's "The Thuringian War" and the multiple stories of her life can be found in *Sainted Women of the Dark Ages*, edited and translated by Jo Ann McNamara, John E. Halborg, and Gordon Whatley. The translation of Teresa of Avila's work I used is by J. M. Cohen. Marie Bonaparte's discussions of Teresa can be found, among other places, in Georges Bataille's *Erotism*.

PART TWO

Bataille's comments about the gospels are from *Guilty*, translated by Bruce Boone. My discussion of Lawrence was also aided by William J. Diebold's *Word and Image: The Art of the Early Middle Ages, 600–1050*. My thinking about Bartholomew, early anatomy, and images of the ecorché was helped by *Books of the Body: Anatomical Ritual and Renaissance Learning*, by Andrea Carlino; *The Body Emblazoned: Dissection and the Human Body in Renaissance Culture*, by Jonathan Sawday (who argues that cadavers should participate in their own dissection); and Leo Steinberg's essay "The Line of Fate in Michelangelo's Painting." The historian who remarked that flaying marked "abhorrence of breaches of the fundamental bond of human society" is W. R. J. Barron in his essay "The Penalties for Treason in Medieval Life and Literature," which I found quoted in Sarah Kay's essay, "Original Skin: Flaying, Reading, and Thinking in the Legend of Saint Bartholomew and Other Works." The Ovid translation I used is by Mary M. Innes. Much of the history of World War II trophy skulls I first learned about through James J. Weingartner's "Trophies of War: U.S. Troops and the Mutilation of Japanese War Dead, 1941–1945."

PART THREE

My discussion of early pornography comes largely from two books: Walter Kendrick's *The Secret Museum* and *The Invention of Pornography, 1500–1800: Obscenity and the Origins of Modernity*, edited by Lynn Hunt, particularly the essay by Paula Findlen. Mishima's *Confessions of a Mask* is translated by Meredith Weatherby; more on the history of artwork about Sebastian can be found in Franco Mormando's *Piety and Plague: From Byzantium to the Baroque*. My copy of Athanasius's life of Anthony is translated by Robert C. Gregg, and Foucault's *History of Madness* is edited by Jean Khalfa and translated by Jonathan Murphy. Thomas Laqueur's *Solitary Sex* offers an enormously useful and comprehensive history of masturbation. In addition to Frederick Brown's *Flaubert: A Life*, biographical details also came from Francis Steegmuller's *Flaubert and Madame Bovary*. The translation of *Madame Bovary* I quote is by Geoffrey Wall; W. G. Sebald's *After Nature* is translated by Michael Hamburger.

PART FOUR

The history of spontaneous human combustion I relate borrows from work done by an excellent essay by Warren S. Walker titled "Lost Liquor Lore: The Blue Flame of Intolerance." John Heymer's theories on the matter can be found in his book *The Entrancing Flame*. Material on Saint Foy, including firsthand accounts of her miracles, can be found in *The Book of Sainte Foy*, translated and edited by Pamela Sheingorn;

Notes on Sources

Hannah Green's *Little Saint* is also excellent. And though the priests Green talked to in the late 1970s maintain that Foy's bones were not stolen, a detailed account of the theft of her relics can be found in Patrick Geary's *Furta Sacra*, on which I relied for my account. The history of Saint George in England is detailed in depth in Jonathan Good's *The Cult of St. George in Medieval England*; his influence in the Middle East is described in William Dalrymple's excellent *From the Holy Mountain*. The translation of Dante I used is Robert and Jean Hollander's; their notes were also extremely helpful, as was John Freccero's book *Dante: The Poetics of Conversion*. The quoted letters from Van Gogh are translated by Arnold J. Pomerans.

Part Five

Heloïse and Abelard's letters are translated by Betty Radice. More information on the Skoptsy cult can be found in Laura Engelstein's *Castration and the Heavenly Kingdom: A Russian Folktale*. My discussion of crying benefits from Tom Lutz's excellent *Crying: A Natural and Cultural History of Tears*. For Margery Kempe's writings, I used Lynn Staley's edition; the essays accompanying her edition of the text were also quite useful in the writing of this book. Robert Glück's book *Margery Kempe* is well worth seeking out.

Acknowledgments

This book could not have been written without the help of a number of people. From the start, (the explosive) Barbara Galletly was an enormously enthusiastic supporter of this project, and this book would not have happened without her ideas, encouragement, and friendship.

Many thanks to Mark Allen and Michele Yu at Machine Project in Los Angeles and Amaranth Borsuk and Bryan Hurt of the Loudest Voice reading series for hosting the early readings that became this book. Joanna Ebenstein, founder of the Morbid Anatomy Library in Brooklyn, also hosted some early talks and has been a constant friend and sounding board for advice and ideas. Endless thanks as well to the wonderful people at *Lapham's Quarterly*, particularly Timothy Don, who was invaluable in securing image permissions for the book, and Michelle Legro, for reasons too numerous to mention. Thanks also to Susan Lester, M.D., for patiently answering many of my weirder medical questions.

Perpetual thanks to Libby Jordan, Rachel Kinbar Grace, Caitlin Hamilton Summie, Rich Rennicks, and the rest of the wonderful team at Unbridled Books. And deepest thanks once again to Fred Ramey, whose editorial advice and support made this book what it is.

COLIN DICKEY is the author of *Cranioklepty: Grave Robbing and the Search for Genius*. His work has appeared in *Lapham's Quarterly, Cabinet, TriQuarterly* and elsewhere. He is also co-editor—with Nicole Antebi and Robby Herbst—of *Failure! Experiments in Aesthetic and Social Practices*. A native of the San Francisco Bay Area, he lives in Los Angeles.